Revival
OR JUDGMENT?

Which Will You
Choose for Our Country?

BOB FRALEY

® 2013
Robert R. Fraley
All rights reserved
ISBN: 978-0-615-80801-7

Published by
Christian Life Outreach
P.O. Box 31129
Phoenix, Arizona 85046-1129
Phone: 866-998-4136 or 480-998-4136
E-mail: xnlifeout@yahoo.com

Web-site: www.bobfraleychristianlifeoutrach.com

Printed in the United States of America

Design by Robin Black, www.InspirioDesign.com

ABOUT THE AUTHOR

Christian leader and author **Bob Fraley** defines America as the country God raised up to be Salt and Light—the center of Christianity—in these Last Days. But just as Satan often caused the Jewish nation to fall away, he now has his eyes set on destroying "Christian America."

For more than forty years, Bob's books and booklets have helped believers understand the spiritual warfare being waged in America, with over two million copies distributed.

In 1969, God called Bob and his wife, Barbara, to raise six children along with their own after the children's parents were killed in an automobile accident. Today their family flourishes, including seventy-six children, grandchildren, spouses, and great-grandchildren (and growing!). Aside from those too young, they have all made commitments to Jesus Christ as their Lord and Savior.

Then in 1971 a revolutionary experience with the Lord launched Bob on a life-long investigation into the prophetic times in which we now live. It has been the foundation for him and his wife for raising godly children in our increasingly ungodly society. Their remarkable true-life story of how the Lord has led their family the last forty years was recently published in the book, *The Blessings of Obedience*.

Bob is also a successful businessman, having helped develop one new manufacturing company and then starting his own company in 1997. Both companies produce high-tech extruded aluminum alloys for the aerospace industry.

He and his wife have founded several Christian ministries including Campaign Save Christian America; Paradise Valley

Christian School and Mom's Pantry, a community food bank, both in Phoenix, Arizona; Help the World, an outreach to the poor and needy in Kenya, East Africa; and Golden Eagle Christian Center, a Christian retreat center near Greenville, Ohio.

Tommy Barnett, Senior Pastor of Phoenix First Assembly of God, one of the largest churches in America and founder of the Dream Centers wrote, *"Bob Fraley's great love for America has caused him to pen several outstanding books and booklets that have been read by hundreds of thousands. If you ever have an opportunity to read one of his inspiring books, I urge you to take advantage of it. He is a man of life-changing insight."*

Dr. David Mains, Director of the "Chapel of the Air" for twenty years and winner of the 1995 National Religious Broadcaster Programmer of the Year award wrote, *"What Bob Fraley has to say is like a spiritual hand that grabs your backbone through your stomach and shakes you around a bit. I see his words as a great gift for which all of us should be thankful. I believe that through his words you will sense that he walks with the Lord and has certainly been given a message from Him for the greater Christian public."*

ACKNOWLEDGEMENT

I acknowledge and thank our close friend Robert Motsinger for his editorial review and suggestions for this book, which helped bring life to its message.

I acknowledge and thank Dr. David Mains for writing a fifty-day Spiritual Adventure for me based on my book *You Are Salt & Light*. I have revised some of the material from this Adventure and used it for the writing of this book.

CONTENTS

INTRODUCTION

The message of this book can transform your spiritual life and commitment. It has the potential to galvanize God's people to join in His work and to magnify His glorious name by bringing about personal and corporate revival in churches throughout our nation. True greatness is not related to size or spiritual prominence. It is doing God's will. The Lord alone is our Savior, and we are to live for Him.

This message is about far more than forgiveness and Heaven. This world has false standards, false values, false gods, and false heroes. Our calling is to put a kind hand on the shoulder of this world and turn it to seek the face of God.

This book is part of a campaign to save Christian values in America. Hopefully, it will impart new spiritual strength, energy, and vigor into your heart. Its content is drawn from personal experience, thought, meditation, study, and the Holy Spirit's guidance.

By the end of this book, I believe you will have experienced accelerated, measurable, and lasting spiritual growth. By accelerated, I mean growth that is faster than you would normally expect. It's measurable because you will be able to see in your own life how God has aided your progress. And it is lasting because you will form new habits that can stick with you for a lifetime.

As we search the Bible, it has been interesting to me that God always reports the flaws and failures of His people, including His most prominent spiritual leaders: Samson, Saul, David, and Solomon are familiar examples.

The Old Testament consistently reports how the nation of Israel would fall away and later be restored. When God came to Earth in human form—as Jesus Christ, the Messiah—the vast majority did not recognize Him.

Being open and honest—exposing negative things—is normally contrary to what we humans want to hear or deal with. However, that attitude is not consistent with what the Bible teaches us about the ways of God. This leads me to consider some important spiritual issues in our day that need to be addressed throughout the Body of Christ. We do not want to hide our heads in the sand as we draw near to the second coming of Christ, ignoring what prophetic scriptures tell us about our day, just as the Jewish people did at His first coming.

WHAT IS GOING ON IN OUR COUNTRY?

In this last generation, we have experienced an overwhelming increase in the spirit of permissiveness and selfishness **in the Christian community**. Christian leaders, as well as church members, are falling into sexual sin. Addiction to pornography has reached epidemic levels. The overall divorce rate is over fifty percent. Moral actions that were unthinkable thirty or forty years ago are now quite commonplace. An example would be the way unmarried couples have no conscience when it comes to living together outside of marriage. Dishonesty and "shading the truth" runs rampant. I could go on and on, but I don't think that's necessary.

Have you wondered, "What is going on in our country?" It's almost as if there is an unstated national effort to distance ourselves from our religious roots, along with a new emphasis on tolerance that seeks to redefine "Christian America" as a term that's outdated, embarrassing, and—to some—even offensive.

Our government has taken actions that never would have been considered by earlier generations. The most obvious example is the Supreme Court ruling that legalized the killing of more than fifty million innocent babies to date under the appearance of preserving a woman's right to choose—death masquerading as life and freedom.

WE ARE LIVING IN ONE OF THE MOST DIFFICULT TIMES.

We are living in one of the most difficult times that a Christian committed to biblical standards has ever faced. The devil has never enjoyed a better opportunity to tempt people as he does today. No longer does he have to lure us to some dimly lit part of town to show us his wares. Now he boldly comes into our homes without an invitation or even a knock at the door.

Never in the history of mankind has a world system had so much power to teach so many people and advance its standards as our society does through the mass communication systems of TV, radio, movies, the Internet, books, magazines, and our secular educational system are examples familiar to everyone.

Our enemy's evil enticements are conveniently available, and all too often, Christians find his offerings attractive. We are being hit daily in every way imaginable and constantly encouraged to bend and compromise biblical standards.

The America in which we live has become the epicenter of a spiritual war-zone, and many Christians have become statistical casualties, suffering major defeats in their lives. Dr. Billy Graham stated a few years ago that according to his research, at least ninety percent of the Christian population in America is living defeated spiritual lives. The fruit being produced in what was once called "Christian America" would confirm that his findings are probably quite accurate. It is painfully obvious that the Body of Christ is no longer fulfilling one of its most important missions. No longer are we the *"salt of the earth,"* preserving the good in our nation, and serving as the *"light of the world"* (Matthew 5:13–14), leading the way to seek and live in righteousness.

> AMERICA IS
> THAT GEOGRAPHICAL
> RESOURCE CENTER.

Why this has happened is one of the things you will discover as you read this book. In addition you will learn how our enemy has been able to conduct such an effective campaign of spiritual warfare, insidiously overwhelming untold numbers of Christians in our country during the last several decades, just as it was recorded in prophetic scripture.

This book has two key objectives:

1. To help you understand the root cause of *why* the moral fiber of our country has deteriorated so rapidly.
2. To teach you *how* to develop the necessary spiritual foundation to successfully overcome as a Christian during this biblical period of time the Bible describes as the Last Days.

Prophetic scriptures clearly warn that God's enemy, Satan, will conduct all-out warfare against the central resource area of Christianity in these Last Days. America is that geographical resource center. Seeing that his time is short, Satan will try to destroy America's Christian heritage and influence. Again, let me repeat that we need to take seriously and learn from what happened to Israel on so many occasions, because Satan was able to lead them away from living for God, even though they were privileged to be called His chosen people.

We not only need to know about this present-day spiritual warfare going on in our country, we also need to understand Satan's plan of attack so we can properly prepare. Like it was in the days of Noah, we need to build an ark of safety in order to have any chance of surviving these Last Days. Our ark will not be a physical ark like the one Noah built; rather, it will be a spiritual ark. As you read through this book, you will learn why you need this spiritual ark, and how to find and requisition the spiritual building materials needed to build your "ark of safety" for these Last Days.

OUR PERSONAL EXPERIENCE

In 1969, the Lord directed my wife, Barbara, and me to take six children into our home to raise along with our boys after the children's parents had been killed in a tragic automobile accident. We were obedient to this call and, shortly thereafter, the Lord began to do many miraculous works in our lives.

As an example, three of the children were in the accident. Two were okay, but one, ten-year-old Andrea, suffered a fractured skull. The brain damage was so severe that hospital personnel announced she had no chance of survival. They didn't even clean her up from the accident—that job was left for the mortuary.

Andrea's medical records support and confirm that she was miraculously healed. Of course, Christians had been praying for Andrea's survival, and it was obvious who did the healing as the doctors wanted to operate but never had the chance. The amazing thing about this story is that Andrea also had a malfunctioning kidney from the time she was born. She had continuously been under a doctor's care and was often sick, and at ten years of age

The Fraley's 50th wedding anniversary in 2007 with their nine children. The three men in the back right are Bob and Barbara's biological sons. The other six they took into their home as their own in 1969 after the children's parents were killed in an automobile accident.

weighed only forty-one pounds—about half of what a normal ten-year-old should weigh.

But when the Lord healed Andrea's injury from the accident, he healed her completely ... including her malfunctioning kidney. Her frequent visits to the doctor became a thing of the past, and she quickly became a strong, robust child, her weight doubling to eighty-two pounds the first year. Today, she's thriving. She and her husband, along with their four boys, own and operate a large dairy farm near Phoenix, Arizona.

This next example of the Lord's hand being involved in this calling to raise these six children has more to do with the main message of this book.

At the time Barbara and I took them in, we were fairly young, so we became very dependent on the Lord to carry out such a task.

The Lord was faithful to help us by opening our spiritual eyes to see the heavy spiritual warfare the enemy would be waging against Christian values in our country.

That was in June 1971. Because of it, I began to research and study this warfare and write about what I was discovering. My first book was published in 1975. My understanding has grown over the years as the Lord has continued to spiritually refine us. I continued to write and have

WE BECAME VERY DEPENDENT ON THE LORD.

now had eight books and several small booklets published.

What the Lord began to show us forty years ago, what I have written about, has come true. God's enemy has been dragging down Christian leaders, shattering Christian homes, destroying Christian values, and attacking the foundation of our nation. That is why I believe the Lord has continued to inspire me to teach and write, to help equip believers that they may spiritually survive and even excel in these end-times.

The spiritual warfare conducted by our spiritual enemy has caused the moral standards in our country to deteriorate more in the last forty to fifty years than in all the previous years since our forefathers founded America. In the history of mankind, there has never been a society whose moral values have deteriorated so drastically in such a short period of time, and this trend shows no sign of stopping. In fact, the statistics show things are getting worse.

Hebrews 11:7 reads, *"By faith Noah, when warned about things not yet seen, in holy fear built an ark to save his family."* **In a way, this has been our experience** as well. As the Lord warned us of things that were going to be happening to the Christian values in America, **we believed His warning.** He then used scripture to equip us with the materials necessary to build the spiritual ark that would save our family in these difficult days of raising godly children in an increasingly ungodly society.

We now have seventy-six in our immediate family, including our own three boys, the six children the Lord added after the accident, spouses, grandchildren, and great-grandchildren. Everyone who is old enough has made a commitment to serve the Lord Jesus Christ. Both Barbara and I strongly believe that the primary reason for this is that by faith we believed what God warned us about more than forty years ago and how He led us during this time. The spiritual principles we have learned from scripture *work* and have stood the test of time during this period when our country's moral values have deteriorated so dramatically.

> PROPHECY IS ONE OF THE MOST IMPORTANT TOPICS TO UNDERSTAND IN THESE LAST DAYS.

In a recent book, *The Blessings of Obedience: Our Story of How God Has Led and Blessed Our Family*, we share our personal testimony of walking with the Lord and following these spiritual principles over the last forty years. And in another recent book called *You Are Salt & Light*, I summarize all my previous books, covering my research and study of the important spiritual principles the Lord taught us about living the Christian life during this difficult period of time in our nation's history. These books contain scriptural, practical, and prophetic insights that will aid you in building your own spiritual ark during these end-times.

Prophecy is one of the most important topics to understand in these Last Days. The book you are now reading will help you see current events and the future in light of what the Bible actually says—and will encourage you to be busy about the Lord's work while there is still time.

This book will make the prophecies of scripture come alive in new ways—focusing attention on a fascinating subject and pointing to the Bible for answers to questions such as:

- What does the Bible really say about America in these Last Days?
- Who (or what) is the beast of Revelation 13?
- What will eventually happen to the Church?
- How will spiritual warfare unfold in these Last Days?
- How can we bring a God-sent revival for America?

The answers to these questions and many more are contained in the pages of this book. I am not interested in providing you a feel-good spiritual high that leaves your spiritual health unchanged. My earnest expectation is that this effort will bring forth a meaningful and life-changing experience.

This expectation is based on my heartfelt belief that the innate importance of this particular subject matter will quickly become apparent and will easily make up for any shortage of literary genius on my part as an author.

> THIS EFFORT WILL BRING FORTH A MEANINGFUL AND LIFE-CHANGING EXPERIENCE

This literary effort is not intended to be just another study, per se, of the Book of Revelation, but it *does* scrutinize a variety of specific passages. I also venture back into the Old Testament book of Daniel, which is the prototype for all prophetic writings in scripture.

Finally, I want you to join me and begin to pray that the message of this book will serve the objectives for which it was written. And don't forget: After you have finished this book, invite your friends and relatives to share its message. It will be an exciting time for them, as well as for yourself and your church.

ONE

—◊—

OUR MISSION

Jesus proclaimed: *"You are the salt of the earth. But if the salt loses its saltiness, how can it be made salty again? ... You are the light of the world. A city on a hill cannot be hidden. Neither do people light a lamp and put it under a bowl. Instead they put it on its stand, and it gives light to everyone in the house. In the same way, let your light shine before men, that they may see your good deeds and praise your Father in heaven"* (Matthew 5:13–16).

Americans have taken the Gospel of Christ throughout the world and raised up numerous ministries to meet the various needs of people. Even as God obviously had a hand in America's past, He challenges His Church today to be "salt and light" in our present troubled society. In Matthew 5:13–14 Jesus makes two of the most penetrating statements about Christians found anywhere in scripture: *"You are the salt of the earth"* and *"You are the light of the world."* **Jesus gave us our perfect mission statement in these two short sentences.**

> **JESUS GAVE US OUR PERFECT MISSION STATEMENT.**

In our society today, they require a lot of courage to live out and are quite demanding. However, our Lord is saying that Christians are the only people in this world who can preserve the good (our function as salt) and live in righteousness with the under-standing to help in those areas that matter the most (our function as light). **What a challenging and fulfilling adventure Christians are to have in this life on Earth!**

Satan's overall objective is to keep you and me from fulfilling our Lord's mission of being "salt" and "light"—especially in these Last Days. It is important to understand the spiritual warfare in America as these days unfold. The many ways our world system can now con-stantly tempt us has taken its toll. The fruit being produced in the lives of Christians reveals many spiritual defeats are taking place.

WE FACE A GREAT DANGER OF BECOMING CONTAMINATED.

For Jesus to use the word "salt" to describe one of the key functions in the life of a Christian is amazing. Only the wisdom of God could have known what we do today about salt. It is one of the most stable compounds on Earth. On its own, it will *not* lose its saltiness. Salt becomes inef-fective only when it becomes contaminated. This occurs if it is mixed or diluted with some other material or chemical.

To *not* lose its effectiveness, salt has to remain essentially dif-ferent from the medium in which it is placed. When kept in a pure condition, it only takes a small amount of salt to accomplish the purpose of adding flavor or acting as a preservative. If God's people remain in a pure state, it will only take a few of us to make a major difference. History records this happening in the first century dur-ing the beginning of the church.

"But if the salt loses its saltiness, how can it be made salty again? It is no longer good for anything" (Matthew 5:13). Jesus is teaching a principle of life here. If Christians assimilate something other than the purity of God's Word, we face a great danger of becoming

contaminated. Our influence in this world is only effective if we are distinctively different. *"What does a believer have in common with an unbeliever? What agreement is there between the temple of God and idols? For we are the temple of the living God. As God has said: 'I will live with them and walk among them, and I will be their God, and they will be my people …' 'Therefore, come out from them and separate,' says the Lord. 'Touch no unclean thing, and I will receive you'"* (2 Corinthians 6:15–17).

Mixing the standards of the world with God's standards is one of the major temptations the enemy is using today. It causes Christians to become contaminated and lose our "saltiness." It is vital to our mission that we understand what being *"the salt of the earth"* entails. We must be a preserver of the good.

Jesus then proclaimed that Christians are *"the light of the world."* The world is in a state of darkness, even though its people are always talking about their enlightenment. There are many verses that confirm this truth.

> **ONLY CHRISTIANS HAVE BEEN BROUGHT INTO THE LIGHT.**

- *"For he has rescued us from the dominion of darkness and brought us into the kingdom of the Son he loves"* (Colossians 1:13).
- *"For you were once darkness, but now you are light in the Lord"* (Ephesians 5:8).
- *"But you are a chosen people … a people belonging to God … who called you out of darkness into his wonderful light"* (1 Peter 2:9).

Only Christians have been brought into the light. The people of the world remain in spiritual darkness.

The world does not recognize its darkness, however. One of the catchphrases of the Renaissance in the fifteenth and sixteenth centuries was that "knowledge brings light." Many replaced the knowledge of God with man's reasoning, placing human insight above God's revealed wisdom. They replaced the worship of God with the worship of man's intellect.

Mankind does not realize that our knowledge has only increased our understanding of *things*—science, biology, commerce, pleasure—not the *real factors* that are critical to the makeup of a successful and peaceful life. This is why the world's vast accumulation of knowledge has only brought us to the many predicaments we see around us. We humans have failed in the most important area of all. We do not know how to use our knowledge for a more peaceful and happier way of life. Scripture makes clear that it is the Spirit of God and the Word of God that enlightens mankind **with the wisdom** we need to understand and apply what knowledge we have.

Look at the failed relationships between people and nations. We don't seem to understand that **knowledge only gives us the ability to analyze. It does not give us wisdom, or clearly define the right course to follow.** Jesus taught that Christians should give off this light that the world so desperately needs.

Scripture is clear where our wisdom is to come from. Let me quote you just a couple of verses:

- *"Where is the wise man? Where is the scholar? Where is the philosopher of this age? Has not God made foolish the wisdom of the world?"* (1 Corinthians 1:19)
- *"For the wisdom of this world is foolishness in God's sight ... The Lord knows that the thoughts of the wise are futile"* (1 Corinthians 3:19–20).

The world does not have light, because Jesus alone is the light of the world: *"I am the light of the world. 'Whoever follows me will never walk in darkness, but will have the light of life'"* (John 8:12). Only Christians can reflect the light and life of the Son of God. When a person is born-again into His spiritual Kingdom, the Spirit of Jesus Christ begins to live in and through that individual. *"Don't you know that you yourselves are God's temple and that God's Spirit lives in you?"* (1 Corinthians 3:16)

WE REFLECT THE NATURE AND CHARACTER OF HIM.

Christians are **not** the light of the world because of who we are, but because we reflect the nature and character of Him who now lives in us by His Spirit. Jesus said, *"This is the verdict: light* (meaning Himself) *has come into the world, but men loved darkness instead of light because their deeds were evil. Everyone who does evil hates the light, and will not come into the light for fear that his deeds will be exposed. But whoever lives by the truth comes into the light, so that it may be seen plainly that what he has done has been done through God"* (John 3:19–21).

As the light of Jesus Christ shines through us, it exposes the error of man's way of thinking. That is why the Pharisees and scribes, who supposedly had all the answers, hated Jesus so much. It is why the people of the world today, who still think they have the answers, hate many of the teachings found in scripture. **Such a light exposes the sins of mankind with a form of truth so perfect that it cannot be ignored or denied.**

Salt describes our state of *being*, and **light** describes our state of *doing*. Jesus Himself was the perfect manifestation of these two words, which also describe our mission. He did not have the attributes most people would consider necessary to accomplish great things.

He lived in poverty and was reared in obscurity. He never received a formal education, never possessed wealth, and never traveled extensively. Yet in just three and a half years of ministry, the effects of His life on mankind were greater than that of anyone else in history. Once each week, the wheels of commerce ease their turning, as multitudes gather to pay homage to Him. He was God on Earth in the form of a human being. He truly proved that it only takes a small amount of light to make a major difference in a dark world. And the same Spirit that lived in Him lives in every born-again Christian.

It is every Christian's duty to be His ambassador by fulfilling God's mission to be *"the salt of the earth"* and *"the light of the world."* However, according to Bible prophecy, there will be tremendous spiritual warfare initiated by the enemy in the Last Days of the Church Age to keep us from fulfilling our mission. God has given us scriptures about the future so that we will have an accurate insight into how the enemy will carry out this warfare. *As you travel through this book, the enemy's tactics are exposed, so you can* **prepare yourself ahead of time** *to overcome his schemes of deception in these Last Days.* It has been recommended that I emphasize these last two sentences by repeating them. God has given us scriptures about the future so that we will have an accurate insight into how the enemy will carry out this warfare. *As you travel through this book, the enemy's tactics are exposed, so you can prepare yourself ahead of time to overcome his schemes of deception in these Last Days.*

Our problem today is not one of intellect. The Bible tells us it is our sinful nature. Sin is integral to who we are (Romans 5:12 and 7:14–25). In its fallen, sinful state, the world can be a rotten, foul, and polluted place. Left alone, it would probably self-destruct. It needs a preservative and a light that shines brightly, showing forth the love of God. Jesus stated that Christians are that preservative and that source of illumination. No one else is capable of fulfilling these two functions, regardless of how educated they may be or how hard they try.

Fulfillment of our mission to be *"the salt of the earth"* and *"the light of the world"* is an exciting challenge, but it does not happen just because the words are spoken.

There must be a continued audit of the fruit of any mission statement—otherwise, how can you know if it is being fulfilled?

In these Last Days, we are living in one of the toughest times ever to be salt and light—especially in America! There has never been a society with as much power to teach its standards as this

> **THERE HAS NEVER BEEN A SOCIETY WITH AS MUCH POWER TO TEACH ITS STANDARDS.**

society now has. That is one of the reasons God warns us often about the ways of the world. It is one of the enemy's main attack vehicles, tempting Christians and polluting their purity. He knows that compromising with the standards of the world will cause harmful contamination and weaken our ability to function as *salt and light.* I think this must be one of the reasons we find scriptures like: *"You adulterous people, don't you know that friendship with the world is hatred toward God? Anyone who chooses to be a friend of the world becomes an enemy of God"* (James 4:4). *"Do not love the world or anything in the world. If anyone loves the world, the love of the Father is not in him. For everything in the world—the cravings of sinful man, the lust of his eyes and the boasting of what he has and does—comes not from the Father but from the world"* (1 John 2:15–16).

A study of this word "world" in these scriptures is what we call society. It is those things and systems developed by mankind without regard for God's approval. The Bible warns us that the systems mankind has developed are controlled by our spiritual enemy. *"We know that we are children of God, and that the whole world is under the control of the evil one"* (1 John 5:19). Of course, just as man can be converted out of the world into the Kingdom of God, so can the things of the world be converted for the glory of God.

Scripture tells us we are to live *in* the world, but not to be *of* the world. That is because spiritually we are no longer citizens of the kingdom of this world—this world is not our home—we have become citizens of the Kingdom of God. When we bow to Jesus Christ as our personal Savior and Lord, we experience a spiritual rebirth by the power of the Holy Spirit. From that point on, we are no longer a part of the world's spiritual family. Colossians 1:13 states, *"For He has rescued us out of the darkness and gloom of Satan's kingdom and brought us into the kingdom of His dear Son"* (The Living Bible).

This is why the apostle Paul considered the things of this world dead to him and himself dead to this world. He said, *"May I never boast except in the cross of our Lord Jesus Christ, through which the world has been crucified to me, and I to the world"* (Galatians 6:14).

Satan has successfully used his kingdom—the world, or society—in America during this last generation as an attack vehicle to weaken our resolve and contaminate our spiritual commitment. It has affected the Christian community's ability to succeed in preserving the godly standards that the majority in our society has lived by since the founding of our nation. Satan's use of his **kingdom** has made us ineffective as *"salt"* and had a dimming effect on our *"light,"* thus preventing us from carrying out God's mission.

Later I will be discussing a few of the verses from Revelation 13, one of the key prophetic chapters regarding the Last Days. This is referred to as the Last Days spiritual warfare chapter. Let me now briefly point out one of the prophecies made in this chapter about this warfare against Christians in the end-times. It reads, *"Also it* (referring to the "beast") *was allowed to make war on the saints and to conquer* (overcome) *them"* (Revelation 13:7 RSVB).

The word *"conquer"* as used in this verse means to defeat or subdue as one army would do to another, just as we did to Germany and Japan in World War II. It does not mean to obliterate or eliminate. I stated earlier that according to Dr. Billy Graham's research, ninety percent of American Christians are living defeated spiritual lives. That means most of us are not fulfilling God's mission of being *"salt"* and *"light."* It is not that we don't know the Christian

DECEPTION IS A TERRIBLE THING.

thing to say, but our actions or our fruit has been broadcasting our weakness to the world and at least some degree of agreement with its standards. That is, deception!

Deception is a terrible thing. One of the greatest warnings Jesus gave about the Last Days had to do with deception. He said, *"For false Christs and false prophets* (teachers) *will appear and perform great signs and miracles to deceive even the elect—if that were possible"* (Matthew 24:24). There is only way I know of to test deception. That is by inspecting the fruit produced and comparing it with the teachings in the Word of God.

One of the objectives of this book is to focus on the urgency of the times. We do not want to be lulled asleep by the enemy and ignore the implications of the end-time prophecies we will be looking at as we prepare for the **second coming** of Jesus. The Jewish people were guilty of that in the years prior to the first coming, which resulted in a majority who were not ready and actually missed His identity.

Our ignoring biblical teachings and the signs of the times has already brought an enormous amount of spiritual defeat among Christians as dishonesty, sexual permissiveness, divorce, addiction to pornography, greed, and more has exploded to epidemic levels. These defeats will not only increase but worsen if we don't prepare for what's ahead. The church's influence on the world will grow weaker and weaker, and the moral standards in our country sink lower and lower.

In the future, Satan's attacks could well involve persecution, but for now we must deal with the attacks that have caused the greatest distortion of our identity as salt and light, which primarily have come via **deception**. As I have said before, the only way for any of us to really recognize deception is an examination of the fruit of people's lives.

> SPIRITUAL VICTORY IS FOUND IN THE POWER OF THE HOLY SPIRIT.

So what is our answer? How can we regain the effectiveness of the two main functions of Christianity—to be the *"salt of the earth—preserving the good"* and the *"light of the world—living in righteousness"*?

If our contamination has come by way of the world's influence or from the society in which we live, then the most obvious and logical answer is to be less worldly.

That statement has some value, but I can tell you that applying that answer alone will not give you the spiritual victory you seek. It has been tried by many people, and it simply doesn't work. It's not nearly enough.

When people try to develop spiritual things on their own, all that usually happens is that they create a list of rules, doctrines, and regulations they can accomplish in the flesh using their own willpower. This approach may soothe our conscience and even deceive us into thinking that we are having spiritual victory. However, through the years those who have put their faith in such things as a source of spiritual victory have never really succeeded in preserving the good— being the salt—and living a life of righteousness—being the light.

We are talking about a product of the Spirit, not of the flesh. The only source of spiritual victory is found in the power of the Holy Spirit. That is why Jesus said that all of our problems begin with the heart. The heart is where we must start if we are to be victorious over the influence of this world. And I am not talking about salvation. If you are spiritually born-again, you have salvation, and as a result have experienced some life-changing experiences. **What I am addressing here is our delivery from the heavy influence of Satan's kingdom, this world,** which over the last generation has become so powerful that it has overwhelmed and contaminated Christians almost everywhere in our country. The real answer is the same one that has worked in the past and can work again. It is a Spirit-led-revival throughout America.

As we now begin the spiritual adventure presented in this book, we must first take a look at some of the prophetic scriptures foretelling the events that took place in America during the last generation. We will then spend some time discussing revival: what it means and how every Christian can be part of its happening. My goal is to inspire you to choose revival, not judgment, for our country.

TWO

—∞—

LIVING WATCHFULLY

John 21:25 states, *"Jesus did many other things as well. If every one of them were written down, I suppose that even the whole world would not have room for the books that would be written."*

That is a powerful statement! Through John, God makes very clear the extent of Jesus' works. If everything Jesus said and did was recorded, John says, the whole world would not have room to hold all of the books.

According to this verse, only a small amount of what Jesus said and did was recorded. This should tell us that the words and actions of Jesus that God did choose to include in the Bible must be extremely important.

It is a commonly held belief, at least among Christians, that the many end-time prophecies that have already been fulfilled provide proof that we are living in the Last Days of the church age, and very near the time when Jesus will return.

Jesus did not say a whole lot about the Last Days, or if He did, God chose not to record it in scripture. As a consequence, it is logical to assume that God places a tremendous amount of importance on what He did record about our day—and, therefore, so should we! In this chapter, I will discuss a few of those things Jesus warned would occur.

In Luke 17:26–30 Jesus warned us of one of the ways Satan would attack Christians in our time. He said: *"Just as it was in the days of Noah, so also will it be in the days of the Son of Man* (referring to the time of His return). *People were eating, drinking, marrying and being given in marriage up to the day Noah entered the ark. Then the flood came and destroyed them all. It was the same in the days of Lot. People were eating and drinking, buying and selling, planting and building. But the day Lot left Sodom, fire and sulfur rained down from heaven and destroyed them all. It will be just like this on the day the Son of Man is revealed."*

WHY WOULD HE WARN US ABOUT THE NORMAL, EVERYDAY AFFAIRS OF LIFE?

Jesus makes a profound statement in this prophecy that immediately got my attention. Did you notice it? There is something missing in what He said about the days of Noah and Lot. He doesn't mention the many gross sins that were taking place in the days of Noah and Lot. Not one thing that He does mention is within itself a sin. Likewise, He does not say anything about the many gross sins taking place in our day. He only lists the everyday normal affairs of life: eating, marrying, buying, selling, planting, and building.

The Old Testament scriptures state that in the days of Noah and Lot lawlessness, permissiveness, and rebellion were running rampant. This is given as the reason why God had to destroy both of those societies. Similarly, we know that a lot of these same evils exist today. Read any newspaper or listen to any newscast. Yet when comparing our day to those of Noah and Lot, Jesus makes no comment about this fact. Instead His comparison is with the everyday activities of buying, selling, eating, drinking, marrying, planting, and building. Since His comparison refers to the time in which we live, I felt compelled to understand what He meant by His comments. Why would He warn us about the normal, everyday affairs of life?

I think what I discovered will interest you as much as it did me. The answer is more important than we may realize. It leads us to the very core of the spiritual warfare now taking place in our country. It is one of the reasons why the moral values of our society have deteriorated so quickly. *Looking into the future, Jesus could see that deterioration, so He warned us of the cause ahead of time. The importance of that warning is further emphasized by the fact that God had it recorded in His Word.*

This warning from Jesus comparing our day to Noah's is a warning that carries a much deeper and far greater concern than the many gross sins that ordinarily command our attention on a daily basis. Jesus did not have to mention them specifically, because Christians and non-Christians alike are already aware of them. We hear and read about them every day. As an example: The late David Wilkerson, the well-known pastor of Times Square Church in New York City and one of our country's more prominent spiritual leaders of the past stated:

"I was listening to a special radio program in a large eastern city, where the people on the street were being interviewed about the moral condition of America. The question was asked, 'Do you believe America has lost its moral integrity?' Almost all who were interviewed said basically the same thing: 'America is going to hell in a hand basket!' 'We no longer care if scoundrels run our country, as long as we prosper.' 'Morality and purity have been sold out to pleasure and prosperity.'"

God gave us this prophetic warning regarding these Last Days, because He recognized the danger associated with over-commitment to these seemingly harmless everyday affairs of life—the buying, selling, building, and so forth. It is not our involvement in these things that makes them sinful. Our sin is one of over-commitment to the self-serving affairs of everyday life, which has caused an ever more diminishing commitment to live by the standards of God. That apparently was a problem in the days of Noah, and it obviously is a problem today, especially in America. Our relentless pursuit of every-day affairs has become more important to us than our desire to comply with God's moral living standards.

> OUR SIN IS ONE OF OVER-COMMITMENT TO THE SELF-SERVING AFFAIRS OF EVERYDAY LIFE.

Jesus is telling us that in the days of Noah and Lot, the every-day affairs of life became so important to people it caused them to abandon their commitment to place God first and honor His values. Serving God was not their primary focus. He is warning us this same temptation would also be predominant in our day.

It is almost impossible to describe the power our society has acquired in recent years to influence our behavior through highly-developed advertising campaigns, a constant flow of attractive new products, beautiful shopping malls, easy credit, often with no down payment, and a mass media system that delivers that advertising into our homes and everywhere we go. It constantly tempts us to over-commit our time and money and compromise our moral values, so we are encouraged to serve ourselves more than we desire to serve God.

God looked ahead and prophesied through Jesus how our lives would be dominated by these everyday affairs of life. He knew this was one of the reasons why people were led astray in the days of Noah and Lot. They would not listen to Noah and recognize the signs of the times. In His love, He has warned us in the same way.

Understanding this fact should serve as a wake-up call to Christians. God knows that anyone having such a strong commitment to the everyday affairs of life—that our society is now able to develop within us—can easily grow cold in our personal resolve to live by His biblical

> **IN HIS LOVE, HE HAS WARNED US.**

standards. It is a form of deception that Satan is using to destroy "Christian America" in these Last Days, just as Jesus prophesied.

Please don't misunderstand what I am saying. It is not wrong to be materially blessed by God; I know my wife and I have been. However, I can tell you most of the material blessings we received from the Lord came after we were tested for several years to prove that our heart's desire was to obey and put God first in all things, regardless of the sacrifice. At one time in our life, we literally had to walk away from almost everything we had. I tell you this to describe our own unique experience without trying to imply that yours must be the same.

Our first major test of obedience came in 1969 when we were called to take those six children whose parents had been killed in a car accident. Over the next two-and-one-half years, following the Lord's leading for our family required giving up the beautiful new house we had built on fifteen acres and resigning from my corporate executive position, giving up a company Cadillac and many other perks. Then, in obedience to the Lord, we moved our family by faith 2,250 miles across the country without any prospects of a job, facing complete separation from our church family, friends, and relatives. **It basically required us to give up everything we had—to put the Lord first and live by faith following His leading.**

But these years of trusting obedience were followed by many fruitful years of His blessings, including the salvation of our family, which now totals seventy-six and is still growing; the Lord inspiring me to write several Christian books and booklets; teaching and being called to be an elder in a local church; founding several Christian ministries, including a Christian school and recently a community food bank in Phoenix, a Christian Retreat Center in Ohio, and an outreach for the poor and needy in Kenya, East Africa. After moving to Phoenix, I also was blessed in my business life, helping to build a successful manufacturing company, and then starting my own company that became quite successful, both of which produce high-tech aluminum alloy extrusions for the aerospace industry.

So the blessings of this life can properly follow in a life of faith. But this prophecy of Jesus comparing the people in our day to the people in Noah's day addresses our attitude and commitment. Which is more important: the gifts or the God who gives them? In the time of Noah, people paid little or no attention to Noah's message or the signs of the times as he tried to warn them that the things of God must come first. You can almost hear them saying, "Don't bother us, Noah. We're good citizens; we have to take care of our everyday affairs." Genuine repentance and a need to prepare for what was ahead did not seem urgent or even necessary.

The downhill slide of righteous standards in our society in recent years has passed the point where God's values are a major influence in the everyday life of many Americans. That was not true before World War II. Before that time, the standards Christians lived by set the tone for the character of the nation, even though many of the people were not practicing Christians. It was not until after the war, when we became the greatest superpower in the history of mankind, that people began to change.

The worldly standards that have been promoted during this generation in "Christian America" have become **so** *strong and far-reaching* that we cannot hope to avoid the effects of the warfare in which we are involved. The devil has never enjoyed so many opportunities to

> AT NO OTHER TIME IN HISTORY HAVE CHRISTIANS FACED ATTACK ON SO MANY FRONTS.

tempt people as effectively as he does today by utilizing our mass communication system.

At no other time in history have Christians faced attack on so many fronts, having to deal with such means and continuously tempted with the standards and ways of the world. Satan's evil enticements are made conveniently available, and all too often, we find his offerings irresistible. And we have been encouraged to think his ways are harmless.

An important lesson for us to learn is that our values of righteousness can only be compared to God's standards, which never change. As the world's values have drastically deteriorated in recent years, only managing to maintain the same distance between our values and the world's means that our values have also deteriorated. That is why many of the more worldly values of twenty to forty years ago have now become an acceptable living standard for so many Christians.

"I am not as bad as the world" is not an acceptable thought for Christians. It is a deception that leads us to compare our standards with the world's rather than comparing them only with God's. Deception breeds compromise, and compromise leads to spiritual defeat. This graph illustrates what has happened in our country and the underlying reason for the downward slide of Christian standards.

BIBLICAL STANDARDS NEVER CHANGE

WORLDLY STANDARDS   20-40 Years   CHRISTIAN STANDARDS

Are you beginning to see why the God-given prophecy of Jesus, comparing the days of Noah to our day, was recorded in scripture? Over-commitment to the everyday affairs of life has caused the majority in our society, including many Christians, to ignore or pay very little attention to the signs of the times. Therefore, almost nothing has been done to guard against the deceptive spiritual warfare that Jesus and others prophesied would take place in our day. The fruit produced by the body of Christ during the past generation proves this statement to be true.

The enemy is using the influence of our modern-day worldly society to attack Christians, and it is working! Far too many have lost most of their ability to discern right from wrong and are unaware of the things Jesus warned us about. He said in Matthew 24:24 and Mark 13:22 that even the elect (Christians) would be deceived in our day. The truth of this prophecy is difficult to swallow, but the "spirit of merchandising" has captured the heart of most Americans far beyond what might be considered normal over the history of mankind.

I will repeat: The capability of our society to produce so many consumer products, along with the highly skilled advertising that constantly focuses our attention on these products; a media system that delivers this advertising right into our homes; easy credit, often with no down payment; and beautiful shopping malls, have come together to make this prophecy a present-day reality.

God is faithful. He has put these words of warning about our day in the Bible. He knew how important it would be for us to know the kind of spiritual warfare the enemy would use to tempt us in these end-times. We must be careful and constantly alert lest we also develop a strong self-centered attitude about our everyday affairs. It is a strong temptation that is capable of deceiving our hearts, keeping us from developing a strong commitment to live by God's holy standards, growing spiritually, and effectively fulfilling God's mission to be "salt" and "light."

> **THE ENEMY'S DECEPTIVE ATTACKS HAVE BEEN VERY DIFFICULT TO DISCERN.**

The enemy's deceptive attacks have been very difficult to discern in our modern-day world. Our lack of concern and apathetic attitude regarding the many *sins that are now out in the open in our society* are a revealing fruit of this deception. We need to examine the fruit or actions of our lives *compared with God's Word*. This is the only way to determine whether the enemy has deceived us. **Many Christians have become victims,** suffering discouraging spiritual defeats, and are probably unaware of how they are being attacked—or that spiritual compromise is contributing to their fruitless struggles.

The reason I became aware of the spiritual warfare we are experiencing within our society is because of a transformational encounter I had with the Lord in June of 1971, when the Lord opened my spiritual eyes and allowed me to see the warfare that would be taking place in our country as the enemy sought to destroy "Christian America" in these Last Days. This powerful encounter with the Spirit of God has been a driving force ever since, inspiring me to constantly research and study the Bible about the end-times. It was about a year later when I was inspired by the Lord to begin writing and teaching about this subject. Not being a writer, it took me three years to finish my first book, which was published in 1975.

As I grew in my understanding, through research and the study of God's Word about this spiritual warfare, I continued to write and have now written eight books and several small booklets on this subject. My last major book, *You Are Salt & Light*, summarizes the important spiritual principles covered in many of my previous books.

It was the Lord revealing to me the meaning of prophecy about a "beast" in Revelation 13 that caused me and my wife to begin seeking the Lord's direction regarding the way we should live and raise our family in these Last Days. After this encounter, we have tried to always walk by faith with a holy fear. We believed what the Lord showed us about this present-day spiritual warfare, and the facts confirm as truth the reality of moral decline in our country during the past generation.

Earlier, I made a comment about a key verse in Scripture that my wife and I can identify with. The verse is found in Hebrews 11:7. It states, *"By faith Noah, when warned about things not yet seen, in holy fear built an ark to save his family."* The Lord directed Noah to build a physical ark, or a boat, to save his family from the consequences of sin in his time. Likewise, in our day we were led to build an ark, not physical like Noah's, but a spiritual one.

The Bible says the thing that kept Noah on track while building his ark was his faith in what he had heard from the Lord, along with a holy fear that inspired obedience to what the Lord had called him to do. That summarizes our walk over the last forty years.

Another place in scripture where Jesus warned us about end-times is found in Matthew 24. In that passage, He said there are going to be difficult days in the Last Days. There will be false prophets, persecution of believers, signs in the heavens, and great distress in the world. Let me also quote one short paragraph from Matthew 24, because there is a key word in these verses that we need to thoughtfully consider and consciously embrace:

"Therefore keep watch, because you do not know what day your Lord will come. But understand this: If the owner of the house had known at what time of night the thief was coming, he would have kept watch and

KEEP WATCH.

BE READY.

would not have let his house be broken into. So you also must be ready, because the Son of Man will come at an hour when you do not expect him" (Matthew 24:42–44).

For those who are alive near the time of His second coming, Jesus is saying, "Keep watch. Be ready." He is speaking to all of us!

The key word I want you to remember is "watch": "Pay attention." In this same content we tell our children, "Be sure to watch for traffic whenever you cross streets."

The huge Webster's Encyclopedia Unabridged Dictionary of the English Language consists of 1,800 plus pages and lists twenty four different shades of meaning for "watch." These range from the casual "let's watch television" to the important assignment of a soldier: "Yes, sir, I understand my job is to keep the fourth *watch* of the night."

I firmly believe Jesus intended that we should be alert in watching for predicted signs. In the Olivet Discourse, found in Matthew, Mark, and Luke, Jesus detailed specific conditions that would foreshadow His return.

His words will sound familiar. Nation will rise against nation, kingdom against kingdom. There will be famines and earthquakes in various places, and terrors and great signs in the heavens, and so on.

All of these items are characteristic of virtually any historical period—meaning war, famines, and earthquakes are not unique to our time. I assume if Jesus expected these to be special warnings as the time of His second coming approaches, a marked increase of such occurrences would begin taking place.

Questions for us to consider then are:

- Is world famine being talked about more today or less?
- Does it appear that violence and lust have multiplied or decreased?
- How should we respond when a Harvard expert on the subject of earthquakes observes that in the last six centuries, the frequency of earthquakes has increased more than **two thousand percent**?
- Are tornadoes, hurricanes, and violent storms on the rise?
- Is it fair to say that when compared with past generations, the Gospel is now being spread around the world more than ever? Isn't this just one more sign of the Last Days?

How about the sign of the times found in 2 Timothy 3:1–5 where Paul said: *"But mark this, there will be **terrible times in the last days*** (emphasis added). *People will be lovers of themselves, lovers of money, boastful, proud, abusive, disobedient to their parents, ungrateful, unholy, without love, unforgiving, slanderous, without self-control, brutal, not lovers of the good, treacherous, rash, conceited, lovers of pleasure rather than lovers of God—having a form of godliness but denying its power."*

This is particularly interesting because these are characteristics that have evolved during this last generation, especially among Christians. **Paul is talking specifically about Christians** in these verses. Could this possibly be the reason why he calls these days *"terrible times"*?

Jesus also mentions other biblical signs of a different nature that we should watch for. For example, we are to keep watch on the nation of Israel. Here's a country that went out of existence almost 1,900 years earlier, and now it is reborn! In the long history of the world, NEVER has there been anything like this. This is definitely a specific sign that was prophesied as a Last Days event.

To be even more specific, consider the fact that the city of Jerusalem is now under Jewish control. Then read the words of Jesus in Luke 21:24 that clearly predict Jerusalem will be *"trampled on by the Gentiles until the times of the Gentiles are fulfilled."* When these things begin to happen, Jesus said to *"look up and raise your heads because your redemption is drawing near."* We need to watch carefully so that we are fully aware of these signs of the times as prophesied in scripture.

We need to watch so we will live in a state of preparedness. If Jesus were to return today, tomorrow, or any time, we want to be sure there would be no regret whatsoever on our part. Rather, He should find us doing, to the best of our ability, what we know pleases Him.

Another reason we need to watch is so we will carry with us the "unquestioned hope" we have in our eternal destiny. At this particular moment, this may seem a bit abstract to those of us who live in America, but to so many throughout the world, it would have great meaning.

Throughout history, fellow Christians have paid dearly for identifying with the true King, Jesus. Unfortunately, around the world today persecution and imprisonment is already a fulfilled sign of the end times for thousands and thousands of believers. Are you aware that *there were more brothers and sisters in Christ's family martyred for their faith in the twentieth century than in all the previous centuries combined?*

WE HAVE ALLOWED THE ENEMY TO GAIN THE MOMENTUM.

You and I hear the word "watch" in a comfortable sanctuary and then drive home or visit our favorite restaurant to have a Sunday meal together with our family. Usually, none of those close to us are missing, at least not because they have been taken prisoner for their faith. But for far too many, the word "watch" means another day with very little to sustain them and more heartbreak to bear. Their only durable possession is an unquestioning hope! Hoping soon and very soon that their great King comes again! For their sake, may that day be earlier instead of later.

Keep this word "watch" that Jesus gave us close to your heart. For when we live watchfully as our Lord instructs us, we will begin to:

1. Be aware of the predicted signs
2. Live in a state of preparedness
3. Carry with us this unquestioning hope

As I close this chapter, let me say that we have allowed the enemy to gain the momentum in the spiritual warfare of these Last Days. Most people have not even recognized the most obvious signs of all, especially here in America. Our hearts have become over-committed to the everyday affairs of everyday life.

To turn this condition around in the body of Christ, we need a Heaven-sent, Holy Spirit-operated revival. We should fervently be praying for such a revival if we want to save biblical values in our country. Revival will be my main focus later in this book.

In the meantime, remember this:

When we live watchfully as our Lord instructs us,
we will begin to experience the joys of personal revival.

Our adventure will now take us into an exploration of some prophetic scriptures about the Last Days that most people find difficult, if not impossible, to understand.

THREE

—ᴍ—

THOSE STRANGE
APOCALYPTIC WRITINGS

We live in a time when the amount of information available to the public has exploded. Individuals who review various statistics have commented it now doubles about every six months. I don't doubt it! Books have become a multi-billion-dollar business. There are about 200,000 new books published every year. In fact, go to your favorite local bookstore and there are so many choices that you must know at least a little about how the books are categorized or you'll be completely overwhelmed.

For example, there's a difference between fiction and nonfiction. And you won't find children's books mixed in with those for adult readers. Histories and sports volumes are not intermingled. There's a separate travel section and also one for religions, which has its own obvious divisions, just as there is for different kinds of books about cooking. In short, to find a particular volume that appeals to you, you want to at least be heading in the right general direction.

The best-selling book of all times, the Bible, is a little like this in that it is divided into various sections, and we'll better understand a particular message within the Bible if we have some understanding of how it is organized. Its sections are not labeled romance, humor, and military. The Bible does contain certain passages about romance and war, and there are a few rather humorous verses, but basically the Bible is about spiritual matters.

Within this broad topic, however, it also has distinct divisions. The most basic division is between the Old Testament and the New Testament—the Old Testament being about events *prior to* the appearance of the long-awaited Jewish messiah. That word "messiah" is Hebrew, and it means "the anointed of God." The same word in the Greek language is "Christ." The actual name of this Christ, or messiah, the anointed of God, is then revealed in the New Testament to be Jesus, from Nazareth in Galilee.

The Old Testament subdivides into three major sections—history, poetry and prophecy.

Except for the first eleven chapters of Genesis, the first seventeen books are all Jewish histories, beginning with Genesis 12 through the book of Esther.

Next, there are five books of Jewish poetry—Job, Psalms, Proverbs, Ecclesiastes, and the Song of Solomon. When *we* hear the word "poetry," most of us think of rhyming words. Hebrew poetry, however, is more parallelism, or the repetition of similar ideas. An example would be the psalms, which we would probably call written prayers that, unlike the way *we* pray, repeat each idea twice. My point is, the psalms certainly don't read like the earlier books of history, and one shouldn't expect to study them in the same way.

The last of the three major Old Testament divisions is prophecy. Once again, these account for seventeen books, starting with Isaiah and continuing through to Malachi. Given a chance, you very well might rename this grouping "sermons," and that's instructive, because we tend to think of prophets as individuals who only predict the future. Some of these Old Testament preachers actually did, but as a group, their message was more often than not a message from the Lord to His people, "Thus sayeth the Lord," than a message predicting the future.

Once again, you don't listen to a sermon with the same set of expectations as you would when attending a history lesson about a nation's kings. Hearing the works of a poet would also change the way you would listen to them being read. So these three divisions—history, poetry, and prophecy—define the various kinds of written material found in the Old Testament.

The New Testament also has three basic divisions. The first division consists of five books devoted to history. The first four of these historical books are short biographies about the life of Jesus. The fifth book recounts early history in the church and is entitled Acts—The Acts of the Apostles.

Next in the New Testament is what normal people would call letters or correspondence. Bible scholars refer to these as epistles. They're written by different authors, the main contributor being Paul. All of his precede the others. They start with his letters to the churches—Rome, Corinth, Galatia, and so on; then to individuals—Timothy, Titus, and Philemon. After that come letters from other important New Testament authors like Peter and John.

Following these letters, there is one more book. It is quite different from the others. It is entitled Revelation—the Revelation of Jesus Christ. Translated in Greek, the word for Revelation is *apokalypsis*. We say "apocalypse," which refers to writings that unveil truths lying beyond the normal scope of human understanding. So this apocalypse, or Revelation, reveals the true meaning of world events and any future ramifications, including the heavenly perspective associated with each one.

To understand the breadth of God's Word, we need to explore "those strange apocalyptic writings." Apocalyptic materials are a literary composition characterized by a particular style that is found only in these types of writings. They can't be read like ordinary history or letters or sermons or poetry. They belong to a specific category of their own, and must be approached as such.

WE NEED TO EXPLORE "THOSE STRANGE APOCALYPTIC WRITINGS."

Allow me to illustrate what I mean. Today we have many contemporary literature categories that would **not** have been familiar to people in earlier times. A case in point would be books we commonly refer to today as detective stories. Film documentaries are another relatively new form of communication, as are websites, cartoon strips, movies, TV, social networks, blogs, novels, and daily newspapers.

However, in a reverse sense, it is widely believed that early Christians understood apocalyptic writings much better than we do. We're not at all accustomed to them, but they were. These "revelations" came out of desperate times when there was a great need for encouragement. However, the writers and readers were forced to communicate in code, because their very lives were often in danger.

The same is true for the Jews living between the brutal 400 years when the Old Testament was completed and before the coming of Christ. Just surviving was extremely difficult during this period.

Now it's fair to say that all apocalyptic writers model their work in one way or another after the prophet Daniel. He is the prototype. Others regularly borrow his themes and symbols. Restated, it is virtually impossible to fully grasp their messages without at least some working knowledge of Daniel's writings. That's also true when looking at the book of Revelation.

By now, you may be wondering, "Why all this background information? What you're saying sounds more like part of the curriculum for a Bible college or seminary class than it does a Christian book."

But this background information is necessary in order to establish the proper context as we explore "these strange apocalyptic writings"—the ones found in everyone's Bible.

This book is an effort to prepare the reader for what lies ahead. It asks you to make a choice between revival and judgment. I like to think of it as a spiritual adventure. According to the dictionary, an adventure is an exciting experience that is sometimes hazardous. So we're obviously not going on a religious pleasure cruise where there is no risk. In my mind, this is an opportunity to experience accelerated, measurable, and lasting spiritual growth. That's what will mark your life if you choose to fully assimilate the contents of this book. That won't happen if you just read the words and ignore the message.

As we begin looking at some of those strange apocalyptic writings, I want you to start familiarizing yourself with some rather difficult passages in the Bible. There are seven of them, to be exact—three chapters from Revelation and four from Daniel.

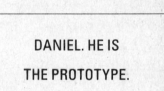

DANIEL. HE IS
THE PROTOTYPE.

First, we are going to read Revelation 1:

"*The revelation of Jesus Christ, which God gave him to show his servants what must soon take place. He made it known by sending his angel to his servant John, who testifies to everything he saw—that is, the word of God and the testimony of Jesus Christ. Blessed is the one who reads the words of this prophecy, and blessed are those who hear it and take to heart what is written in it, because the time is near.*

"*John, to the seven churches in the province of Asia:*

"*Grace and peace to you from him who was, and who is to come, and from the seven spirits before his throne, and from Jesus Christ,* who is the faithful witness, the firstborn from the dead, and the ruler of the kings of the earth.

"To him who loves us and has freed us from our sins by his blood, and has made us to be a kingdom and priests to serve his God and Father—to him be glory and power for ever and ever! Amen.

"Look, he is coming with the clouds, and every eye will see him, even those who pierced him; and all the peoples of the earth will mourn because of him.

"So shall it be! Amen.

"'I am the Alpha and the Omega,' says the Lord God, 'who is, and who was, and who is to come, the Almighty.'

"I, John, your brother and companion in the suffering and kingdom and patient endurance that are ours in Jesus, was on the island of Patmos because of the word of God and the testimony of Jesus. On the Lord's Day I was in the Spirit, and I heard behind me a loud voice like a trumpet, which said: 'Write on a scroll what you see and send it to the seven churches: to Ephesus, Smyrna, Pergamum, Thyatira, Sardis, Philadelphia and Laodicea.'

"I turned around to see the voice that was speaking to me. And when I turned I saw seven golden lampstands, and among the lampstands was someone 'like a son of man,' dressed in a robe reaching down to his feet and with a golden sash around his chest. His head and hair were white like wool, as white as snow, and his eyes were like blazing fire. His feet were like bronze glowing in a furnace, and his voice was like the sound of rushing waters. In his right hand he held seven stars, and out of his mouth came a sharp double-edge sword. His face was like the sun shining in all its brilliance.

"When I saw him, I fell at his feet as though dead. Then he placed his right hand on me and said: 'Do not be afraid. I am the First and Last. I am the Living One; I was dead, and behold I am alive for ever and ever! And I hold the keys of death and Hades.

"'Write, therefore, what you have seen, what is now and what will take place later. The mystery of the seven stars that you saw in my right hand and of the seven golden lampstands is this: The seven stars are the angels of the seven churches, and the seven lampstands are the seven churches.'"

Now that you have read this chapter let me ask you a few questions:

1. According to the first verse, is this a revelation or an apocalypse of Jesus Christ, John, or the church?
2. How was this revelation made known?
3. At what verse does John begin using "visionary language" and for how long?
4. Verse 17 describes John's response to what he saw. How might you have responded?

This chapter gives you what I would call an initial feel for the apocalyptic style of writing. For example, let me again quote verses 12 through 16: *"And when I turned I saw seven golden lampstands, and among the lampstands was someone 'like a son of man,' dressed in a robe reaching down to his feet and with a golden sash around his chest. His head and hair were white like wool, as white as snow, and his eyes were like blazing fire. His feet were like bronze glowing in a furnace, and his voice was like the sound of rushing waters. In his right hand he held seven stars, and out of his mouth came a sharp double-edged sword. His face was like the sun shining in all its brilliance."*

You may recall that the person being described here is none other than the Son of God, Jesus the Christ. You also might recall that the lampstands are the seven churches of Asia Minor that our Lord addresses one by one in Revelation chapters two and three.

The stars, according to verse 20, are the angels of the seven churches, but having that information isn't crucial in terms of understanding this opening chapter. If you weren't told in the text, you could conceivably spend all kinds of time trying to figure out something that isn't really that important to an understanding of the main thrust of this passage. My only point is that one has to be careful with apocalyptic writings, because it is very easy to get bogged down with less important details, only to miss the big picture.

When you have an opportunity, read Daniel 10, which sounds very similar to Revelation 1. I will quote verses 5 and 6: *"I looked up and there before me was a man dressed in linen, with a belt of the finest gold around his waist. His body was like chrysolite, his face like lightning, his eyes like flaming torches, his arms and legs like the gleam of burnished bronze, and his voice like the sound of a multitude."*

Is this the same person that John meets in Revelation 1? Daniel 10 tells us. Once you have discovered the answer to that question, you might want to think about several others like:

- What are the twelve ways Daniel physically and emotionally responded to his vision?
- What else is similar about Daniel 10 and Revelation 1?
- What activity had Daniel been engaged in that precipitated this vision?
- How do you think you would react to an experience like this?

I would now ask you to read Daniel 7 and Revelation 13. Notice how these two passages are connected. They are good preparation for chapters four and five of this book, which I promise will get your attention.

Before I continue, here are some general guidelines to consider as you attempt to decipher apocalyptic materials.

1. **Revelation had historic relevance for first-century Christians.** It was written initially for them, just like Colossians was written for the church in Colossae, the book of Corinthians for the

church in Corinth, the book of Ephesians for the church in Ephesus, and so on. So, when exploring the meaning of Revelation as it applies to us, we can't just ignore its original purpose. What it said to the early church must necessarily be a part of any consideration.

2. **The purpose of the book was to** *encourage steadfast faith during persecution.* If I say the word persecution in the presence of the typical American, he hears it in his head, but does not feel it in his guts. Domitian was the Roman ruler during the time in which the book of Revelation was penned, and he was second only to Nero in terms of his cruelty to Christian believers. To him, executions became like sporting events, as did various kinds of torture. I could give specifics but see no reason to include them here. Obviously, John's message from the risen Christ would have been a very great encouragement during such desperate times.

3. **Apocalyptic disclosures characteristically came through visions.** That's important. Look at it this way. If I say to you, "Let me tell you about a good book I just finished," you will listen in a much different way than if I say, "I had the strangest dream last night. Would you mind if I shared it?"

Dreams. Visions. These words instantly inform us we're not talking about a detailed medical lecture on how the human body functions. Instead, we would expect to hear about angels and other strange beings of a wholly unfamiliar world.

4. **Grasping the overall picture is far more important than mastering the small details.** I touched on this previously. But I mention it again, because I know that many are compelled to tie up each and every loose end as they encounter them. For these individuals, not doing so is like solving the most difficult parts of a crossword puzzle or sudoku and never completing it. Apocalyptic writings are a different kind of puzzle—one that can only be completed by God Himself. We can be certain, however,

that in the end true justice will prevail. Good will triumph over evil, and Jesus will reign as Lord over all.

5. **Visions don't always unfold in chronological order.** Respected Bible scholar John Stott writes:

"The visions are chronological, but the events represented in the visions need not be so. John saw one vision follow another. But it is not necessary to suppose that the visions reveal a historical sequence. They are successive visions of Christ. They are not visions of successive events. Many of the visions portray the same period, the Christian dispensation, which stretches from the first to the second coming of Christ, but each has its different emphasis or insight. The book is not a film showing the continuous unfolding of one story but a series of … slides depicting the same landscape from different angles."

6. **The primary guideline for understanding the mysterious imagery of apocalyptic writings has its roots in the writings of Daniel.** As you read Daniel 7 and Revelation 13, you will quickly see the truth of this statement.

7. **Symbols, along with certain numbers, have a very unique meaning.** The writer tells you exactly what some of his symbols represent. For example, the dragon is Satan. Conversely, the lamb is always Jesus.

Here's Revelation 5:6–8: *"Then I saw a Lamb, looking as if it had been slain, standing in the center of the throne, encircled by the four living creatures and the elders. He had seven horns and seven eyes, which are the seven spirits of God sent out into all the earth. He came and took the scroll from the right hand of him who sat on the throne. And when he had taken it, the four living creatures and the twenty-four elders fell down before the Lamb. Each one had a harp and they were holding golden bowls full of incense, which are the prayers of the saints."*

There's another symbol—golden bowls full of incense, which

are the prayers of the saints. Without help would we have gotten that one right? Probably not.

Also, the seven eyes are the seven spirits of God sent out into all the earth. I don't think John means for us to try to picture the seven eyes and where they fit on the lamb's face. Rather, the number seven is the number used throughout the Bible to mean completeness or sometimes perfection. As used in this verse, it represents the perfect vision of the lamb that is able to see everything that is taking place, everywhere, in real time.

8. **The vantage point of the narrative can shift from earthly to heavenly.** Let me cover this quickly. Sometimes it can be helpful as we try to understand apocalyptic writings to ask, "Does this passage view what is going on from man's perspective or from God's?" Both perspectives are a possibility.

9. **Cosmic catastrophes characterize a number of Bible passages.** As you read apocalyptic materials, you encounter earthquakes, floods, the sun being darkened, the moon turning to blood, and the sky rolled up. What's literal and what's figurative? Again, this is visionary language. What's being described is the Earth as we know it going through convulsions—a concept that is not entirely unique to apocalyptic writings.

In this regard, here are the words of Jesus in Luke 21:25–28: *"There will be signs in the sun, moon and stars. On the earth, nations will be in anguish and perplexity at the roaring and tossing of the sea. Men will faint from terror, apprehensive of what is coming on the world, for the heavenly bodies will be shaken. At that time they will see the Son of Man coming in a cloud with power and great glory. When these things begin to take place, stand up and lift up your heads, because your redemption is drawing near."*

10. **The last guideline is: It takes some time to get your mind acclimated to such an unusual approach.** That's why I

said earlier—to understand the breadth of God's Word, we need
to *explore* "these strange apocalyptic writings." We will be doing
just that in this book—exploring some of these passages, getting
more familiar with them.

Personally, I think it's nothing short of remarkable that God
would include this approach in His written Word. Just look at
how it begins in Revelation 1:1: *"The revelation of Jesus Christ,
which God gave him to show his servants what must soon take place.
He made it known by sending his angels to his servant John."*

Down through the ages, this approach has proven to be a
comfort to persecuted believers and a literature for the oppressed.
It has also kept Christians absolutely intrigued with what the
future might hold. And how does God pull this off? He gives us
a book that in many ways is mysterious, while at the same time
makes enough sense to intrigue and thoroughly engage the best
of Bible scholars in serious study. Is it even possible that this can
be anything other than a message from the Lord?

So we're off on our Adventure! In chapters four and five of
this book, you will read about the beast who comes out of the sea
in Revelation 13. These are two of the key chapters in this book.
He has *"ten horns and seven heads, with ten crowns on his horns,
and on each head a blasphemous name."* He resembles a leopard,
but he has feet like a bear and the mouth of a lion.

The dragon, or Satan, gives this beast his power, his throne,
and his great authority.

The text says that men worship the beast and ask, *"Who is like
him? Who can make war against him?"*

In chapters four and five, I will discuss, in detail, just who or
what this beast might be. As with all apocalyptic writings, you
should anticipate discovery and stand ready to embrace legitimate
truth when it becomes apparent.

FOUR

—‹‹‹—

THE ENEMY'S DECEPTIVE WAYS

S atan has been known to masquerade as an angel of light. Therefore, we would do well to recognize our enemy's deceptive ways.

Let me ask you a question: Have you ever been blindsided?

I don't know of anyone who likes to be blindsided! Fights are bad enough, but to attack someone when they aren't expecting it is the way a coward does things.

In a similar manner, it is very difficult for any of us to deal with deception—with someone whose word can't be trusted. A child,

> JESUS DESCRIBES
> THE DEVIL AS BOTH A LIAR
> AND A MURDERER.

friend, or spouse who lies to you repeatedly does great damage to whatever closeness you might like to have.

Murder, of course, is an even greater offense. We hear in the news about killings so often that we become numbed to the awfulness of what's being reported. To take the life of another human being is a terrible act. Both the state and the church condemn it.

Jesus describes the devil as both a liar and a murderer. He means this literally. Listen to what He says in John 8:44: *"He was a murderer from the beginning, not holding to the truth. When he lies he speaks his native language, for he is a liar and the father of lies."*

These are sobering words. Many people in this so-called enlightened age think it is weird or even silly to believe in the devil. However, Jesus recognized Satan as not only real, but as a tough and
terrible enemy.

THE DEVIL IS CLEVERLY DECEPTIVE.

I, too, believe there is a Satan.
He's not the red-faced cartoon devil
with horns, hoofs, and a three-
pronged pitchfork. The Satan that
scripture reveals as the Prince of the
Power of the Air is for real. He's the one who tried to deceive Jesus
and sidetrack Him as He traveled the difficult road to Calvary. Ultimately, Satan failed, but he did succeed in another incredibly important area of conflict, which I will discuss a little later.

In similar fashion, Satan tempts us to live contrary to God's
desire. I don't believe Satan has a body like we do, so he's not going
to come up and put his arm around us. The Bible depicts him as
a fallen angel and also as a spirit, like the one that entered Judas
Iscariot. The devil is not omnipresent like God, but he has many
subordinates who carry out his commands. They are spirits also,
as depicted in the Gospels when Jesus cast out demons. Though
they didn't have bodies, their presence was definitely sensed. And
many of us have had times when we, too, have sensed the very
presence of nearby evil.

We can learn quite a bit from scripture about Satan's character. For example, he is highly intelligent … proud … rebellious
… violent … revengeful … corrupting … and, when given the
chance, dominating.

The skill I would like to focus on, however, is the one I brought
up at the beginning of this chapter: The devil is cleverly deceptive.
He's cunning. To repeat Jesus' words, *"Lying is his native language."*
And because he is very good at it, this enemy can never be trusted.

In 2 Corinthians 11:14 the apostle Paul writes, *"For Satan himself masquerades as an angel of light."* Anyone would have to be incredibly skilled to pull this off! But the Bible says he did. In fact, there are many in the world today who actually worship as their god the things of Satan. They don't seem to know it, but in reality he is the exact opposite of God in every way.

To masquerade is to wear a disguise, or to assume the appearance of something you're not. Satan is not God, and Satan is never, ever your friend, though he repeatedly pretends that he is.

His desire is to have millions—actually, I should say *billions*—bow before him. You see this clearly when you read Revelation 13. It's the one where the devil gives his power over to the beast that emerges from the sea.

Using the general guidelines I gave you in the previous chapter, you will immediately realize that this mysterious imagery of a beast has its roots in the writings of Daniel. This is a frame of reference that we don't want to forget. In Daniel 7 we're told that the four terrifying beasts that Daniel saw represented empires or kingdoms. Since the very best resource for interpreting scripture is the Bible itself, it seems logical to conclude that the beast of Revelation 13, having characteristics similar to the one in Daniel, would also represent an empire or kingdom.

> **THE VERY BEST RESOURCE FOR INTERPRETING SCRIPTURE IS THE BIBLE ITSELF.**

Another guideline I gave you in the previous chapter was that the book of Revelation had historic significance for first-century Christians. Based on this premise, it is almost a given that they would have associated this beast with the persecuting power of Rome, governed at the time by the Emperor Domitian, whose reputation for cruelty was topped only by Nero's.

In Revelation 13:11, John mentions a second beast that also appears in the end-times. It differs from the first in that it comes up out of the earth rather than the sea. The fact that John calls it a beast would mean it, too, will be a powerful entity—in fact, the Bible states it exercised all of the authority of the first beast. Other verses in Revelation 13 provide additional details about this second beast, telling us it would be a powerful influence in the society developed under the authority of the first beast. In earlier chapters of this book, we looked at:

- The powerful deteriorating influence of our society on Christian standards in recent years.
- Our individual spiritual commitment to become salt and light.
- The prophecy of Jesus warning us about our over-commitment to the everyday affairs of life as it was in the days of Noah, ignoring the prophetic signs of the time.

THAT FALSE RELIGION IS CALLED HUMANISM.

But one area I have not reviewed is the false religion that has developed in our society since we became the world's greatest superpower. The philosophy of this religion has contributed heavily to the rapid deterioration of our country's moral values. Other verses found in the book of Revelation refer to this second beast as a false prophet or teacher. The three principle entities discussed in Revelation 13 together create what is referred to as an *unholy trinity* consisting of:

1. Satan.
2. The first beast, which is a great political/military/economic world power (what we would describe as a superpower rather than an empire as in Daniel's day).

3. The society of the first beast that develops a false religion that skillfully redefines self-service as a spiritual virtue. That false religion is called Humanism.

Humanism glorifies the individual and elevates him to an equal, or even higher, standing with the creator of the universe. Furthermore, it grants an unrestricted license to decide for ourselves what is right and what is wrong, with no regard for any standard of obedience and faith as set forth in God's Word. The insidious appeal of such a philosophy is undeniable. It is not surprising that the false and deceptive religion of Humanism has swept through our country like a wildfire and is part of Satan's effort to destroy "Christian America."

The philosophy of Humanism embodies the very deceptive nature and character of Satan. It is why God cast him out of Heaven. The prophet Isaiah, speaking of Satan, reports: *"How you have fallen from heaven, O morning star, son of the dawn! You have been cast down to the earth, you who once laid low the nations! You said in your heart, I will ascend to heaven; I will raise my throne above the stars of God; I will sit enthroned on the mount of assembly, on the utmost heights of the sacred mountain. I will ascend above the tops of the clouds; I will make myself like the Most High"* (Isaiah 14:12–14). I will do this, I will do that, I have the right to decide right and wrong, I want. This matches the philosophy of Humanism perfectly.

> HUMANISM HAS SWEPT THROUGH OUR COUNTRY LIKE A WILDFIRE.

Many people are greatly concerned about the increasing influence of Islam. Personally, I find it hard to believe that committed Christians would ever be deceived by it. Revelation 13 states that Satan will tempt Christians using *deception*. **Most Americans,**

Dr. James Dobson

The same twisted philosophy that permits us to kill infants through abortion with impunity is now prevalent throughout the western world. This new way of thinking has produced a society that is extremely dangerous to minds and bodies of children.

including Christians, do not really understand what Humanism is all about and do not equate it with a religion. Focused concerns about its deceptive philosophy simply do not exist.

To give you an example, a survey by Dr. James Dobson's organization Focus on the Family reports that nearly all of the textbooks now being used in our public schools indoctrinate the students with the basic tenets of Humanism. The Christian community may object from time to time to some of the things being taught, but it has never really rallied together in a coordinated effort to voice objections. As a consequence, school leaders often feel free to advocate policies that contradict and even oppose the teachings of the Bible.

Secular humanists have long realized that controlling what young people are taught will ultimately determine the philosophical standards of the future in our society. In this way, they can set an ideological revolution in motion without ever firing a shot. This is definitely one of the reasons why our nation's Christian heritage is being extinguished so quickly. Abraham Lincoln once said: *"The philosophy of the classroom today will be the philosophy of the government tomorrow."* Most of us have been an unsuspecting witness to the fulfillment of his words.

Discussing the contemporary state of American culture, Dr. James Dobson writes:

"The same twisted philosophy that permits us to kill infants through abortion with impunity is now prevalent throughout the western world. This new way of thinking has produced a society that is extremely dangerous to the minds and bodies of children.

"It should be clear that one of our jobs as parents must be to keep these temptation doors closed, locked, and barred to adolescents. It is frightening today to see that these doors are not only unlocked for many of our youth—they are wide open. It is no wonder that the kids who want to remain chaste are often made to feel like prudes and freaks.

"With the heartache and illness the loose humanistic standards are now causing for the families of our society, one would think responsible adults would be united in a campaign in opposition. But normally the contrary is found to be true."

Most Bible scholars agree that in the end times there will be this evil trinity formed between Satan, a powerful political/military/economic world superpower, and a false religion that shows little or no tolerance for the Christian faith or any Christian standard. This conforms to what is described in Revelation 13—a chapter that is often referred to as "the end-times spiritual warfare" chapter.

Will there eventually be an antichrist figure leading this power, or alliance of powers? Certainly that is possible, but such leadership could very well be like the many different caesars who ruled from Rome. Elected officials are even a third possibility. There are different possible interpretations.

At this point, it is important to insert a measure of caution. It is far more important to grasp the overall picture than to be preoccupied with the small details. Given the fact that Satan is described as the great deceiver, I sincerely doubt the beast or superpower of Revelation 13 will appear very beastly as it ascends to power.

> I SINCERELY DOUBT THE BEAST OR SUPERPOWER OF REVELATION 13 WILL APPEAR VERY BEASTLY.

There are only three occasions in the Bible when we hear Satan speak openly. In none of them does he sneak up behind a person and yell something scary. Neither does he growl or roar. He is extremely clever and very shrewd. In the Garden of Eden, he pretends to be an understanding friend to Eve.

Later on when Satan speaks to God about Job, he makes a simple observation: "Job loves you because you bless him. Take away the good life he enjoys and his response to you will be quite different!"

Again, in the wilderness when talking to Jesus, Satan appears quite empathetic in voicing his *suggestions*. You can read about them in the first few verses of chapter 4 of Luke and Matthew. Paraphrasing one temptation, he says to Jesus: "You must be hungry. How long has it been? Forty days. If you're the Son of God, why don't you just turn these stones into bread?"

On each occasion, his use of temptation follows the same pattern. He wants each individual—Eve, Job, or Jesus—to focus on their own immediate needs or wants first before considering the will or standard of God, which by the way is exactly the same philosophy taught as truth in the religion of Humanism.

I have brought these three conversations to your attention, because each dialogue clearly supports my contention that the beast of Revelation 13 will not, in the beginning, make a frightening appearance. Only later, after many Christians have bought into the deceptions from the influence of its society will its evil become apparent. Certainly, this scenario, when compared with scripture, is entirely credible.

If you browse through books written about prophecy, it's not uncommon to find writers who identify this beast, this future empire or alliance of nations, as a modern-day European revival of the old Roman Empire. Some scholars have even suggested that its identity might be related to the formation of the European Union. On the surface, this doesn't seem very deceptive.

THE SUPERPOWER BEING CONSIDERED MUST FULFILL THE SEVERAL DESCRIPTIVE CHARACTERISTICS LISTED IN CHAPTER 13.

There was also a time when another popular theory was being circulated that identified the former Soviet Union as the beast because it was a superpower. As you might expect, that claim usually got an emotional response. Since the collapse of the Soviet Union, however, that theory has faded.

To make a claim as to the identity of the beast in Revelation 13, the superpower being considered must fulfill the several descriptive characteristics listed in chapter 13. Neither of the two I have mentioned comes close. Why I say this will become clear as you read chapter 5 of this book.

We can be relatively certain that this beast is indeed a powerful nation or alignment of nations. We learn that from the book of Daniel. In biblical times, ordinary people didn't use this particular term, but in modern American vernacular, we would call it a superpower—a single governmental entity having a disproportionate influence politically, economically, and militarily throughout the entire world.

At the present, this is an exact description of the global role the U.S. plays. Since the breakup of the Soviet Union, we are undoubtedly the strongest military power on the face of Earth. Economically, we have been predominant ever since World War II. Politically, standing alone or through our alliances, we have a greater say in international affairs than any other nation.

In fact, when you talk to people from other countries, many will point to us, saying as some Arab nations do, "They are the killers! They indiscriminately drop their bombs on civilian targets. These are not just conventional bombs; they have even used big bunker-busters. Is there any other country in the world that has detonated an A-bomb, two of them, over two large cities?"

"America is a fountain of immorality," they continue. "Look at their movies and TV programs. Listen to their music. Tell us who's buying the largest share of the world's illegal drugs. Who supplies the majority of guns and tanks and jet fighters and rockets so that the rest of civilization can blast away at each other? Name the country where greedy people and rich children struggle with a major problem of obesity. It's not us. Don't look this way!"

For the most part, we Americans largely dismiss comments like these because they seem biased and too one-sided. They totally ignore the longstanding reputation of America as the land of the free. We know there has never been another major power in the history of the world more charitable or compassionate to friend or foe in times of need.

After World War II, didn't we rebuild the very infrastructures of the nations we helped defeat? We provided thirteen billion dollars under the Marshall Plan alone. That's *billion*, not *million*, and back then, the dollar was worth a whole lot more than it is now.

Of course that was over sixty years ago, and a lot has happened in the interim. After World War II, we became the greatest superpower in the history of mankind, and soon thereafter, the spiritual values in America begin to change dramatically. Clearly, everything is not the same as it used to be.

This past generation, we have experienced an overwhelming increase in the spirit of lawlessness, permissiveness, and selfishness, even among Christians. Moral actions that were virtually unthinkable a few decades ago are now quite commonplace. Some of these were mentioned in the introduction of this book: Christian leaders indulging in sexual sin; addiction to pornography, even among Christians, at epidemic levels; an exploding divorce rate; rampant crime, violence, and drug abuse; and the largest prison population per capita of any country in the world. In fact, the results of a survey among young American adults showed that the percentage who follow biblically based values as a pattern for living has dropped since World War II from sixty-five percent to a mere four percent.

> AFTER WORLD WAR II, WE BECAME THE GREATEST SUPERPOWER IN THE HISTORY OF MANKIND.

In the history of mankind, there has never been a society whose moral values have deteriorated so dramatically, in such a short period of time, as those of Americans during the past half century, and that trend shows no sign of stopping. Wait a minute ... isn't that a characteristic describing the beast in the second sentence of Revelation 13:2? *"The dragon gave the beast* (this Last Days superpower) *his power."*

Where will we be as a people in another ten, twenty, or thirty years? Is it possible, given the rapid changes occurring everyday in our society, that in these Last Days Satan has deceived our own government to become a willing superpower tool of his to undermine any serious commitment to biblical standards and, thereby, deceive and overcome many Christians? Do these events not square with the prophecies about this beast found in Revelation 13?

Over the past few decades, much has been said about the tremendous inroads the devil has made in our country. Along the way, however, we seem to have been tricked into assuming that the beast/superpower will preside over a society that is much more deceptive and wicked than what we have become. Is it possible we Christians have been blindsided and have swallowed a hoax?

I said earlier that the devil was not able to sidetrack Jesus when tempting Him, but he did succeed in another area of incredible importance—one with which we are all familiar. Remember: The devil comes *only* to steal, kill, and destroy. And whom would he most want to leave destitute?

A huge priority for Satan had to be that of robbing a unique God-given heritage from the Jewish nation. If he could keep them from rejoicing in the wonder of what they would give to the world, that would surely have been a very satisfying victory for him. This would be equivalent to mocking God: "Sure you won, but it cost you dearly."

Knowing that the Son of God would eventually appear on this Earth, but not knowing the specifics, I believe the devil worked overtime to make sure that when Jesus did arrive, the Jewish leaders would respond by saying, "Thanks, but no thanks!"

Scripture declares, *"He* (referring to Jesus) *came unto his own, and his own received him not"* (John 1:11, KJV). This is an incredibly sad verse. The very people of God, the nation uniquely privileged to deliver His one and only Son into the world, were robbed of the joy that should have accompanied such a wonderful event. They literally turned their back on Him.

This should be very frightening, because it shows that a nation that experienced firsthand the earthly presence of God, that witnessed the spectacular miracles and a level of insight unmatched in all of human history, could be completely hoodwinked by this very clever enemy. In denial, they rejected the obvious truth and found no pleasure in the literal presence of their creator. The incarnation of the living God was taking place in real time right before their eyes, and they didn't even know it. Could something like this happen again?

THIS SHOULD BE VERY FRIGHTENING.

Is it within the realm of possibility that the enemy is in the process of deceiving America, in spite of its historically strong Christian heritage, strong Christian teaching, and strong Christian leadership? **Could we be experiencing a modern-day version of what took place within the Jewish nation at the time of the first coming of Jesus?**

Has Satan, masquerading as an angel of light, once again fooled the majority of believers into thinking the beast, or this superpower, has to be a communist government, an Islamic dominion, or some country beyond our shores when, in reality, it's "Christian America" that he has set his sights on?

There is nothing in all of the Bible and nothing about who we are as a people that prohibits the U.S. from becoming backslidden and that very same beast/superpower that John envisioned in the Last days. This would be totally consistent with the way Satan has worked in the past.

And against whom does the beast make war? The answer to that question is given in Revelation 13:7–8. It states:

"He (referring to this beast or superpower) *was given power to make war against the saints and to conquer them. And he was given authority over every tribe, people, language and nation. All inhabitants of the earth will worship the beast—all whose names have not been written in the book of life belonging to the Lamb that was slain from the creation of the world."*

Here the word "conquer" does not mean to eliminate. Rather, it means to overcome and not fulfill the will of God, or refers to not living according to the established standards of God. This has become a real problem in our country and the Christian community during this last generation.

John states the inhabitants of the Earth worship the beast/superpower. This doesn't necessarily refer to a literal bowing-down to the beast/superpower, but could be as straightforward as a feeling of awe toward its power and position in the world. This is very common of people around the world toward America. Having authority over every tribe, people, language, and nation has a similar meaning, suggesting this beast/superpower would be the dominant power in the world.

Equating the American government with the beast or superpower in the Last Days not only makes logical sense when considering the strategies of Satan, it answers several important questions that have continued to puzzle Christian scholars studying Bible prophecy. More specifically, why isn't America found in Bible prophecy? Why would the greatest superpower in the history of mankind and the citadel of Christianity in these Last Days be completely absent? What caused our country's moral values to deteriorate so dramatically in such a short period of time?

It is obvious that once we became the world's greatest

superpower, the rate of moral decay accelerated—more so in this generation than in all the previous years combined since our forefathers founded our country. HOW is this even possible in a land that has more Bible colleges, seminaries, churches, Christian books, tapes, videos, evangelistic outreaches, Christian bookstores, and TV and radio stations than the rest of the world combined? No effort by the Christian community or even secular society, be it new programs, education, laws, you name it, has been successful in stopping this deterioration. Things just continue to get worse! HOW and WHY has our enemy, Satan, been able to effectively undermine so many of our Christian values during this last generation?

HOW AND WHY HAS OUR ENEMY, SATAN, BEEN ABLE TO EFFECTIVELY UNDERMINE SO MANY OF OUR CHRISTIAN VALUES.

As an aside, let me address the answer to this question by sharing in more detail an experience I had with the Lord in June of 1971. I mentioned this encounter earlier. At the time, my wife and I were fairly young and inexperienced, lacking godly wisdom to raise the six additional children the Lord had called us to take into our family in 1969. As a consequence, we became very dependent on the Lord, relying heavily on His direction. In John 15:16 Jesus declares:

"You did not choose me, but I chose you and appointed you to go and bear fruit—fruit that will last. Then the Father will give you whatever you ask in my name."

About a year and a half after taking these children into our home, I had an encounter with the Lord that provided the wisdom we were seeking for the task of raising these children. But I believe it also provides an answer to the question of—WHY Satan has enjoyed so much success in the war on Christian values in our country. It was during this encounter that the Lord revealed the identity of the "beast coming out of the sea" as prophesied in Revelation 13. He showed me clearly that this beast/superpower is what the American government becomes in these Last Days—the greatest superpower in the history of mankind developed here in America, for all intents and purposes the world capital of Christianity.

At that very moment as the Lord identified this beast/superpower, the power of God fell on me in a way I cannot adequately describe. I can only say it literally overpowered me, nearly knocking me to my knees. By faith I believed this revelation came from the Lord. I can't help but think that, because I did believe, the presence of Jesus flooded my soul, and the power of His presence has been with me since that day. The evidence of which, is told through our testimony over the last forty plus years.

Both my wife and I believed this revelation was from the Lord and took it very seriously, even though I had not been studying the book of Revelation or even thinking about the identity of this beast when it occurred.

This encounter was so powerful, it caused me to immediately begin searching the Bible to see if it confirmed what had been revealed. That inspiration has never left. Since then, I have remained faithful spending thousands of hours in research and study over a period of forty years and, along the way, have written several other books and booklets about the Last Days and how they relate to present-day America. One of them, *You Are Salt & Light: Equipping Christians for These Last Days,* includes a verse-by-verse analysis of Revelation 13, along with an accurate interpretation of the Greek text.

My research provided some very convincing evidence showing that since World War II, our government has already fulfilled or begun transformation to almost every descriptive characteristic of the beast/superpower found in Revelation 13. In the next chapter of this book, I explain the strange apocalyptic writings of Revelation 13:1 that list six of those characteristics.

One of the very first things the Lord impressed upon me after my encounter with Him in 1971 was, "KNOW YOUR ENEMY."

Earlier in this chapter, I shared a number of spiritual observations. Perhaps the most intriguing to me is how in just about every competitive situation, be it military, sports, business—you name it—we humans do our best to identify and understand our competition or enemy. Instinctively, we apply this principle whenever we are pitted against a competitor. In our spiritual life, however, this instinct is often ignored or even suppressed.

From the beginning, God has led and blessed America spiritually. A review of our history reveals that His intervention during the formation and spiritual development of our country is historically unique when compared with that of any other, with the exception of Israel. Learning that Satan has always opposed God and His people and tried to sabotage anything God has raised up and endorsed, it should surprise no one that Satan has now launched a savage attack on the remaining biblical values in America during these Last Days. He knows his time is short. Therefore, he has been forced to step up his attack, dragging down Christian leaders, destroying Christian homes, undermining our moral code, and assaulting the spiritual foundation of the entire nation.

This remarkable revelation I had served as a gloomy warning to my wife and me that Christian values in America would soon be the target of severe attacks by our spiritual enemy, Satan. We took that warning seriously, even though, at the time, it was *not* obvious that our country's moral values were going to deteriorate so rapidly. In hindsight, events the last forty plus years provide solid evidence that this prophetic warning actually did originate with God.

When the Lord opened our spiritual eyes to the warfare that would soon take place in our country, it seemed only prudent to make His warning the foundation upon which we were to guide and raise our children. Subsequently, it became the key to spiritual success within our family.

I will again quote Hebrews 11:7 as it best describes our response to the Lord's warning: *"By faith Noah, when warned about things not yet seen, in holy fear built an ark to save his family."* Like Noah, we have conscientiously tried to live our lives with a holy fear and in obedience to the Lord's guidance. We haven't always had the right answer to every one of life's problems. But during these troubling times, we have served as a living example of how to apply this prophetic warning to equip our family and ourselves for spiritual victory. As mentioned earlier, the

> WE HAVE CONSCIENTIOUSLY TRIED TO LIVE OUR LIVES WITH A HOLY FEAR AND IN OBEDIENCE.

true life details of how the Lord led and protected our family have been published in a recent book, *The Blessings of Obedience.*

In 2 Corinthians, the apostle Paul talks about taking a certain action, because he doesn't want Satan to outwit the church. He says in chapter 2, verse 11: *"For we are not unaware of his schemes."* While not wanting to sound presumptuous, may I say that, like Paul, these are my exact sentiments. I don't want anyone to underestimate Satan's cleverness. I repeat: He's very cunning. He's been known to masquerade as an angel of light, so we would do well to be on the alert for our enemy's deceptive ways as **he has always tried to sabotage and destroy anything God has raised up.** Our country's history tells us that God did intervene early and often in the development of America.

As I researched and studied the spiritual development of America, it became increasingly clear that man's wisdom alone did not develop America. It came through men who were inspired by the Lord. Like Israel, the spiritual history of America is

THE SPIRITUAL HISTORY OF AMERICA IS VERY UNIQUE.

very unique compared to that of other countries. Obviously, God has used our people and resources to take the Gospel of Jesus Christ throughout the world and to meet the needs of the poor and needy everywhere. However, with that being said, we can expect that Satan will try to destroy America as a Christian nation. We are now under that attack! I am committed, and ask you to join me, in doing everything we can do to save "Christian America." You will learn how to accomplish this as you continue to read through this book.

Many of our Christian leaders are now proclaiming that America is heading for judgment by the hand of God. Luke 12:48 states, *"From everyone who has been given much, much will be demanded; and from the one who has been entrusted with much, much more will be asked."*

The Christian community has been weakened, but I don't think Christians in America have made so many mistakes that the condition is fatal. However, there is no question that we will be held accountable, and the time has definitely come for the people of God to heed His voice. Later I'll begin to spell out what that means. It will require some changes, but that's to be expected.

So that we don't despair, I am going to close this chapter by sharing Revelation 20:10:

"And the devil, who deceives them, was thrown into the lake of burning sulfur, where the beast and the false prophet had been thrown."

That's the end of the story. The phrase *"thrown into the lake of burning sulfur"* (or "burning fire") means "will be destroyed." As with other apocalyptic writings, it does not necessarily mean a literal fire.

For now, listen to the words of John—this time they come from his first New Testament epistle. Here's 1 John 4:1–4:

"Dear friends, do not believe every spirit, but test the spirits to see whether they are from God, because many false prophets have gone out into the world.

"This is how you can recognize the Spirit of God: Every spirit that acknowledges that Jesus Christ has come in the flesh is from God, but every spirit that does not acknowledge Jesus is not from God. This is the spirit of the antichrist, which you have heard is coming and even now is already in the world.

"You, dear children, are from God and have overcome them, because the one who is in you is greater than the one who is in the world."

And all God's people said ... "Amen."

FIVE

RETHINKING REVELATION 13

Verse one of Revelation 13 is a good example of those strange apocalyptic writings I discussed earlier. It reads: *"And I saw a beast coming out of the sea. He had ten horns and seven heads, with ten crowns on his horns, and on each head, a blasphemous name."*

These prophetic words may seem difficult, if not impossible, to decipher. However, I think you will agree with me as we travel through this verse, its words are actually a blessing from the Lord to keep us from being misled.

After the experience I had in June 1971 that revealed the identity of this "beast/super-power," I researched and studied for over a year trying to determine what these strange prophetic words might mean. Over and over I would have to lay aside any possible candidate, because the peace of the Lord would vanish.

I FINALLY GAVE UP.

After going through this process for quite some time, I finally gave up and told the Lord, "If you want me to understand the meaning of the words and phrases John uses to describe this beast, you will have to tell me." I subsequently put away my research materials and all of my commentaries.

What I am going to tell you next may raise your eyebrows. I want you to know I am only relating what actually took place. Soon after telling the Lord "I give up," the Holy Spirit began to open my spiritual eyes. Over the next few months, the Holy Spirit revealed exactly what these unique prophetic words and phrases characterizing this beast mean. I think you will find it somewhat amazing, just as I did. After being shown, their meaning was quite simple, yet very insightful. Isn't that the way it usually is with the Lord?

Before I continue, I want you to know that I believe in and follow the principle that anything we believe the Lord has revealed to us must be confirmed by scripture. That must always be our test before reaching any definite conclusion.

A careful reading of this verse reveals six distinct characteristics of this beast. Since World War II, our government began the process of fulfilling John's prophecies about the beast in accordance with every detail. No other government system even comes close. For now, I will only consider the first verse of Revelation 13, but first there are some basic guidelines we need to remember when looking at prophetic Scriptures.

1. There is no higher authority for understanding God's Word than to refer to other scriptures where a similar word or phrase is used. This is what Jesus often did. This is the most important guideline, because we are going to the source of that inspiration rather than simply using speculation and conjecture to interpret. If an interpretation holds for one passage, it should for every other as well. What's more, the Word of God is absolutely accurate. We may not always understand everything it says, but we should *not* try to come up with an idea unless it has been documented accurately in the Bible.

2. In order to understand a word or passage, it is often necessary to study the original language in which it was written. The Old Testament was written predominantly in Hebrew, and the New Testament in Greek. Difficult passages often require learning what that word or phrase meant to the Hebrew or Greek author. This is especially true with prophetic words and phrases.

3. Historical evidence either confirms that a prophecy has already been fulfilled or is yet to be. Prophecies are statements about future events. Either they have happened as foretold, or they haven't. Any evidence should be conclusive.

4. Words in prophecy sometimes are used differently than their literal meaning. A word in prophecy may have a symbolic meaning rather than a concrete one. This will become more evident as we proceed.

The Revelation 13 depiction of the beast is one of the most detailed and exacting descriptions in the Bible. Evidently God did not want any mistake with regard to its identity. There are many theories about the identity of this beast, but I couldn't find any that say they have run a scriptural test on each word and phrase to confirm a particular view.

John prophesies, *"And the dragon* [Satan] *stood on the shore of the sea. And I saw a beast coming out of the sea. He had ten horns and seven heads, with ten crowns on his horns, and on each head a blasphemous name"* (Revelation 13:1). If I can demonstrate that since World War II our government begun fulfilling John's prophecies about this beast of Revelation 13, then the enemy has, indeed, come up with an incredibly deceptive method to keep Christians in America from fulfilling our mission to become **the salt of the earth and the light of the world** in these Last Days.

The six descriptive characteristics in verse one are:

1. Beast
2. Coming out of the sea
3. Ten horns
4. Seven heads

5. Ten crowns on his horns

6. On each head a blasphemous name

Characteristic #1: Beast. The actual meaning of the word "beast" as used in prophecy should be abundantly clear. First of all, we need to remember God's inspired Word is the highest authority anyone can use to determine the meaning of anything found in scripture.

Fortunately, the Old Testament prophet Daniel also uses the word "beasts," and he is given the meaning **directly from an angel**. I would encourage everyone to read Daniel 7 in its entirety. But here are some highlights that should help to clarify the exact meaning.

> THE BEAST OF REVELATION 13
>
> IS NONE OTHER THAN
>
> THE GREATEST SUPERPOWER
>
> IN THE HISTORY OF MANKIND.

"In the first year of Belshazzar king of Babylon, Daniel had a dream, and visions passed through his mind as he was lying on his bed. He wrote down the substance of his dream. Daniel said: 'In my vision at night I looked, and there before me were the four winds of heaven churning up the great sea. Four great beasts, each different from the others, came up out of the sea" (Daniel 7:1–3). *"I, Daniel, was troubled in spirit, and the visions that passed through my mind disturbed me. I approached one of those standing there and asked him the true meaning of all this. So he told me and gave me the interpretation of these things: The four great beasts are four kingdoms that will rise from the earth"* (Daniel 7:15–17).

According to the interpretation given to Daniel, the word "beast" in prophetic scripture refers to a kingdom, an empire, or what we would call a superpower. Elsewhere in the Book of Daniel, the four "beasts" he saw are described as the superpowers of Babylon,

Media-Persia, Greece (under Alexander the Great), and the Roman Empire. In the first part of chapter 7, Daniel also describes three of the beasts as wild animals—one as a lion, one as a bear, and one as a leopard. Note that John uses all three of these animals in Revelation 13:2 to describe the beast he saw. This indicates the beast of Revelation 13 is none other than the greatest superpower in the history of mankind. Isn't that a perfect description of what our government has become in this last generation?

Daniel used the word "beast" to describe the major world powers from his time to when Israel is destroyed. John uses the word in the same way when describing the superpower that will rise up in the era of those who give testimony to Jesus Christ in the Last Days, and Israel once again becomes a nation. Our own federal government fully qualifies as a beast in a prophetic sense, because we have obviously ascended to superpower status.

Let me pause briefly to explain something that may be an issue for some of you. The beast of Revelation 13 is thought by several people to be a man. Some Bible translations actually refer to it as a man, while others refer to it as an entity or a superpower. For example, the King James and the first published New International Version used the *masculine pronouns* "he," "his," and "him," when referring to the beast, which suggests that it is a man. The Revised Standard Version, the recently published **revised** New International Version, which was changed to more accurately reflect the Greek meaning, along with the Philips translation and others use the *neuter pronoun* "it" and "its" when referring to the beast, thereby indicating that the beast is actually a superpower, rather than a person.

The *noun* translated "beast" in Revelation 13 is the Greek word *onpiov*.

The Greek word *avrov* is the *pronoun* Revelation 13 uses in reference to the beast. To be grammatically correct, a *pronoun* must be of the **same gender as the noun** to which it refers. If the original Greek word used for beast is **masculine**, then "he," "his," and "him" are the correct pronouns. But if the original Greek word is **gender neuter**, then "it" and "its" are the proper translation.

To properly interpret this word, I asked a friend who was acquainted with one of the top Greek scholars in the country to ask this scholar if it is correct to use the pronouns "he," "his," and "him" when referring to this beast, or is using "it" and "its" the correct approach?

I was informed that the Greek word for "beast" in Revelation 13 is **gender neuter**. This means **"it" and "its" are actually the correct pronouns**. That is a grammatical fact. As a consequence, I am forced to conclude that any publisher using the masculine gender pronouns "he," "his," and "him" when referring to the word "beast" is using an inaccurate translation. Zondervan indicates this in its Greek-English New Testament. (See Greek-English New Testament, Zondervan Publishing House, Grand Rapids, MI, 1975, p. 751.) Let me repeat: The Greek word for beast is *gender neuter*, so "it" and "its" are the proper rendering in John's account. Thus, like Daniel, John very likely used the word "beast" to refer to a superpower, not an individual.

I also asked our son to check this out while he was attending Southwest Baptist Seminary studying for his masters degree of Divinity. He too confirmed the Greek word for "beast" is gender neuter.

Interpreting John's use of the prophetic word "beast" to mean a superpower is also consistent with our very first guideline, which is to rely on other scriptures whenever possible—in this case, the Book of Daniel. Obviously, every superpower had human leaders, even as Babylon did in Daniel's day. But there is still no credible reason to presume that this passage demonstrates a bias in favor of a person instead of a superpower.

Characteristic #2: Coming out of the sea. This phrase also appears in Daniel. So the angel's interpretation of Daniel's vision can also be used to understand John's vision. Daniel writes, *"Four great beasts, each different from the others, came up out of the sea"* (7:3). Daniel's four beasts (Daniel 7:1–7) refer to a succession of world powers that shaped Israel's history before the time of Christ. The lion represents Babylon, which conquered Egypt in 606 B.C. and subsequently achieved political prominence in the Middle East. The bear represents the Media-Persian Empire that overcame the Babylonians in about 539 B.C. and continued to rule until 331 B.C., when Alexander the Great arrived on the scene and defeated them (Daniel 8:21). The leopard represents the Greek Empire under Alexander, which eventually splintered into four separate kingdoms as Daniel prophesied it would (Daniel 8:8, 8:22). The last of these four splintered kingdoms continued until 31 B.C., when, as Daniel prophesied (8:9–12, 23–25), the Roman Empire rose to power.

> THE PEOPLING OF AMERICA IS ONE OF THE GREAT DRAMAS IN HISTORY.

In Daniel's account, a succession of peoples from different geographic bases conquered one another, bringing together people from Africa, Asia, and Europe in a mixture of customs, cultures, and languages. From this historical perspective we can logically infer that *"coming out of the sea"* involves a culturally and ethnically diverse empire or nation. This fits with Revelation 17:15, which reads, *"The waters you saw ... are peoples, multitudes, nations and languages."* As a nation of immigrants, the United States certainly fits this description. Europeans and Africans joined indigenous peoples of North America during the Colonial Period, followed by waves of immigrants from all parts of the Earth throughout the nineteenth and twentieth century's. Together, these people have become modern America—a "nation of nations."

The peopling of America is one of the great dramas in history. Over the years, a stream of humanity crossed continents and oceans to reach the United States. They came speaking many languages and representing almost every nationality, race, and religion. Today, there are more people of Irish ancestry in the United States than in Ireland, more Jews than in Israel, and more people of African descent than in most African countries. There are more Polish people in Detroit alone than in most of Poland's major cities and more than twice as many people of Italian descent in New York as there are in Venice.

DANIEL PROPHESIED ABOUT SUPERPOWERS THAT IMPACTED THE HISTORY OF ISRAEL.

The setting in which the history of these people has unfolded is as impressive as the diversity of the peoples themselves. The United States is the largest cultural-linguistic unit in the world. The distance from San Francisco to Boston is about the same as from Madrid to Moscow. Yet we have one primary language, one set of federal laws, and one economy. This same area in Europe is fragmented into numerous nations, languages, and competing military and political blocs.

The "melting pot" was once a popular image of American assimilation. The largest single ethnic strain is of European ancestry. Together the various homelands of these people formed a region of the old Roman Empire. Daniel prophesied in chapter 7 that another power, a new country, would rise up out of the people of the old Roman Empire. It would become stronger than any of the other powers. He even states that this new power will defeat three of the powers out of the old Roman Empire. It is a historical fact that we defeated England, France, and Spain in our earlier years.

Daniel prophesied about superpowers that impacted the history of Israel. He would have no reason to include a prophecy about any superpower after the Roman Empire and before Israel once again became a nation, which as we know was soon after World War II. Coincidentally, that is when we gained superpower status and we also became an important ally of Israel. How long that relationship will endure is open to debate.

Our country definitely fits the descriptive characteristic of *"coming out of the sea."*

Characteristic #3: Ten horns. Understanding the biblical use of the phrase *"ten horns"* requires an independent interpretation of each word.

Many numbers in scripture have a parallel symbolic meaning that has no relationship to their actual numerical value. Bible scholars have written entire books on these meanings. Such studies have deduced that *"ten"* stands for all-encompassing. Prominent examples of ten in scripture include the Ten Commandments and the ten plagues. In these examples, ten is used to mean an exact count. Numbers in prophecy, however, are often symbolic. For example, in Revelation 12:3, John uses the phrase *"ten horns"* when describing the Roman Empire as a tool of the red dragon—Satan—even though Rome ruled about twenty-seven other nations. Daniel also uses the number *ten* in chapter 7 in a symbolic way to indicate "all-encompassing."

The second word in this descriptive phrase is *"horns."* Throughout the Bible, *"horns"* are a common symbol of strength. In the Book of Daniel, the word represents nations. Presumably, John, too, is using *"horns"* to mean nations. These would be nations with substantial power and influence but less than that of a beast, or a superpower. The beast of Revelation 13 has *"ten horns,"* suggesting this superpower has great influence over several other powerful nations.

The United States is a nation of superpower status. Of course, there are other powerful nations (horns) in the world today. Japan and Germany are economic powers; Russia is still a military power. France and England are former colonial powers that still wield some political influence. But only the United States can legitimately claim to be a superpower. We exercise a considerable amount of economic, military, and political influence over a great many of the world's lesser powers.

ANY INTERPRETATION MUST COMPLY WITH EVERY IDENTIFYING WORD AND PHRASE.

You may be familiar with another popular interpretation of *"ten horns"* contending that they represent the alliance of nations in the European Union. However, the EU *does not* match most all other descriptive phrases in Revelation 13 that pertain to this end-time superpower. To be valid, any interpretation must comply with every identifying word and phrase the Lord has provided. That is why each of these descriptions has been included in the Bible—so we don't have to speculate. Obviously, our present government passes the test of *"ten horns."*

Characteristic #4: Seven heads. The explanation of *"seven heads"* is fairly simple. Seven throughout scripture denotes completeness. God completed creation in seven days. Joshua was commanded to march around the city of Jericho for seven days. On the seventh day, the priests and the army marched around the city seven times. When this march ended, the walls fell. Elisha told the military captain Naaman to dip himself seven times in the Jordan River, and he would be healed. Just as the number ten is used symbolically in prophetic phrases to indicate "all-encompassing," seven is used to denote "completeness."

The word *"heads"* simply means leadership. For John to prophesy that this beast, or superpower, would have seven heads emphasizes the fact that its leadership would not only be complete in all areas of world affairs, but it would also dominate—be number one—in commerce, industrial output, production of goods and services, agriculture, military might, political power, and economic wealth.

"Seven heads" means this end-time superpower will enjoy superiority, or be complete, in all areas of international influence. Since World War II, the U.S. has developed a position in world affairs that easily equates with everything John saw. Are you beginning to see the possibility that this prophecy is really about us?

Characteristic #5: Ten crowns on his horns. Out of all the six characteristics of the beast, or superpower, listed in Revelation 13:1, *"ten crowns on his horns"* is truly unique. It is such a demanding characteristic. The word "crown" (or "diadem" as some versions read) was a distinctive mark of royalty among the early Greeks and Romans. If the word crown or diadem is used, something is being said about its political position.

To use the word crowns with horns indicates this prophetic phrase *is describing the political position of the horns,* or nations, the superpower in Revelation 13 will influence. In summary then, I will break this phrase down. *Ten* means all-encompassing, *crowns* means political position, and *horns* make reference to various powerful countries. When John writes that the *crowns* (political control) were positioned on the *horns* (each nation), he indicates each country will have its own governing political body. So in the Last Days this superpower will allow those nations under its influence to retain political autonomy.

If the superpower described in Revelation 13:1 controlled these other countries politically, then scripture would have said

> THE U.S. IS THE ONLY
> SUPERPOWER I KNOW OF THAT
> SO CLEARLY DEMONSTRATES THIS
> DISTINCTIVE CHARACTERISTIC.

*"ten crowns on **his head**"* in order to reflect the beast's political leadership over them. It would not have placed the *crowns* on each separate *horn* or nation.

The U.S. is the only superpower I know of that so clearly demonstrates this distinctive characteristic. For example, we were instrumental in the defeat of both Japan and Germany in World War II, yet when it was over, we allowed each country to retain its political autonomy even assisting in reconstruction of both countries.

This imagery of *crowns* and *horns*, of politics and nations, is a telling description of our relationship with other nations. America's influence reaches across the globe. Missionaries have journeyed from our shores to the most remote parts of the Earth, and American brand names, TV shows, and popular music are found everywhere. The United States maintains more military bases and foreign embassies than any other nation, and its technological, industrial, and commercial influence are a magnet for an ever-growing portion of the world's population being drawn into its grasp. Almost none of these people, however, owe allegiance to the American flag. Only a relative few of those subjected to this influence are actually U.S. citizens.

How aptly John's phrase of *crowns* and *horns* describes America's influence: Without exception, these nations are heavily influenced by our culture and commerce, but not ruled by our laws. Who can deny that we alone pass this **unique test** God gives to identify this end-time superpower.

Characteristic #6: On each head a blasphemous name. First, we need to examine the word *blasphemy*. Without a proper understanding of the sin itself, it would be difficult to comprehend how it could relate to the *heads* of the beasts or to that aspect of their leadership traits.

Throughout the Old Testament, blasphemy was always considered one of the gravest sins an individual could commit. By definition, to blaspheme is to make light or sport of the name and sovereignty of God. In the New Testament, the Greek word for blasphemy means to injure one's reputation. The scriptures are unequivocal and teach in no uncertain terms that the holy name of God is sacred. To use His name in any way that is not marked with a sense of awe and majesty is viewed as blasphemy.

To better understand blasphemy, think about what happened immediately prior to the Crucifixion. Jesus was in fact true deity, but the Sanhedrin did not accept Him as such, and the high priest condemned Him to death for what was considered blasphemy. The seriousness of this offense is highlighted by the fact that it was punishable by death. So when Jesus publicly acknowledged His deity, the religious leaders were able to charge that he had misused the name of God, or blasphemed.

> TO BLASPHEME IS TO MAKE LIGHT OR SPORT OF THE NAME AND SOVEREIGNTY OF GOD.

In describing the superpower of Revelation 13, John speaks of a blasphemous name on each head. I am certain that this means the leadership of our government will misuse the sacred name of God after becoming a world superpower. John indicates as much when he states that in each area of leadership—each head—of this Last Days superpower will use the sacred name of God irreverently while at the same time, it is carrying out unrighteous acts.

Obviously, this implies that our government will promote a worldly cause while claiming a strong association with God. This is exactly what has begun to happen during the last generation as evidenced by the passing of laws that legitimize and even promote sin. Examples include the promotion of sexual promiscuity in schools as a result of passing out condoms, sponsoring the murder of millions of unborn babies by legalizing abortion, and outlawing public prayer in our public schools.

It is no secret that many of our nation's founders submitted to the Lord's direction. But on our way to worldwide superiority during this last generation, we have largely seen fit to abandon the godly principles of our forefathers. Other governments engage in wicked activities. But no other nation publicly claims God's blessing, while at the same time it commits so much evil. No more needs to be said! We easily pass the sixth test of Revelation 13:1.

If this verse had been written in contemporary English, and the symbols were replaced with their contemporary explanations, it might read something like this:

"And I saw a world superpower develop in a new country made up of people from many nationalities. It influenced other powerful nations throughout the world. It held a position of leadership in every area of world affairs, although it did not try to politically rule other countries—they were allowed to govern themselves. It used the name of God freely and irreverently in many of its worldly activities."

Following, for your convenience, I have included a quick reference definition guide to the strange apocalyptic words and phrases found in verse one that characterizes the superpower of Revelation 13.

- **BEAST:** Empire or superpower
- **OUT OF THE SEA:** A nation of peoples from diverse cultural and ethnic backgrounds

- **NUMERAL TEN:** All-encompassing
- **HORNS:** Nations with significant power, authority and influence, but not superpowers
- **NUMERAL SEVEN:** Completeness
- **HEADS:** Leadership
- **CROWNS OR DIADEM:** A distinct mark of royalty or political position
- **BLASPHEMY:** To diminish the name of God by misusing His holy name

In these Last Days the beast/superpower that Satan gives his complete authority to will no doubt be the greatest superpower this world has ever seen. To me, this scenario makes a lot more sense than one in which the devil forms an alliance with a second- or third-rate power. In addition, as you read Revelation 13, it is going to be in a country where Christianity has been dominant.

Today our government not only holds a position of world dominance, but it also fits all of the descriptive characteristics John used to identify the beast. Therefore, I must conclude our present government is indeed the beast of Revelation 13, as prophesied by Jesus and recorded by John.

This review of verse one was taken from my book *You Are Salt & Light*. In it I scrutinize each verse of Revelation 13, including the wound of the beast from verse 3 and a related personal experience that provides a rather fascinating perspective of its meaning. I spent most of one chapter in that book discussing the history of that prophetic event, the wound of the beast, because it was so thoroughly dramatic, awesome, and inexplicable. It is, in fact, what catapulted us to a position of leadership in the world.

As I conclude this chapter, let me wrap it up by reminding everyone that America was founded on Christian principles. And because

God often intervened in our nation's spiritual development, we eventually became the world's epicenter of Christianity. However, during this last generation, two important changes took place: First, we became the greatest superpower in the history of mankind; and second, despite the fact that there were thousands of churches, thousands of evangelistic outreach ministries, and throughout the land, the Bible was being taught everyday on radio and TV, our moral values deteriorated on a scale greater than all previous years combined since the beginning of our country.

AMERICA WAS FOUNDED ON CHRISTIAN PRINCIPLES.

Knowing that Satan has always been dedicated to the destruction of anything God raises up, should we not at least consider the possibility that our country is playing a role in the Revelation 13 "spiritual warfare" prophecy about the Last Days—that our government is itself fulfilling this prophecy of the beast?

I fear that Satan's ability to deceive is greater than most of us are willing to acknowledge. He is far better at pulling off a sneak attack than most of us realize. Because we have all had some personal experience with spiritual failure, we tend to focus exclusively on the individual. Anyone who has ever been in a position of church leadership knows this same emphasis is also predominant in congregational settings. Only a few seem to realize his evil ambitions also include the nations. American Christians are faced with a decision of unimaginable consequence. They can acknowledge the evidence that has been placed before their eyes, or they can pretend it does not exist. A Christian community that chooses the latter is certain to please the enemy and facilitate his continuing use of the great assets of America for his increasingly evil purposes.

SIX

—ᴍ—

PERSECUTION OF CHRISTIANS IN AMERICA

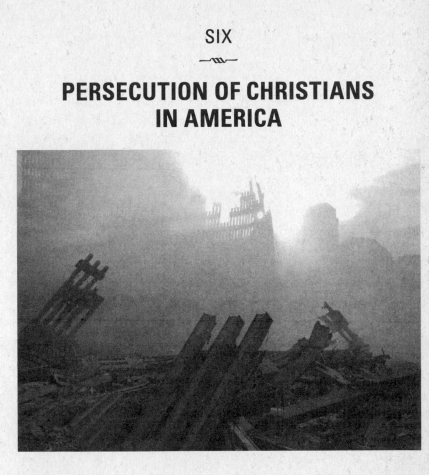

As we continue to explore Revelation 13, Christ's followers should guardedly prepare for the possibility of persecution. Let me ask you: How often do you consider the fact that America, at this very moment, is engaged in two major wars?

No doubt you remember where you were on the morning of September 11, 2001. Millions of Americans were huddled around their television or radio, feeling confused and shocked. Terrorists had attacked America, and we were at war! Over a decade later, we still face the same threat.

However, our country's second war is hardly ever talked about or even understood. Yet, it has the same objective as the first—to tear apart the fabric of our nation and destroy the very foundation upon which America was built. This second war is a spiritual warfare that is being waged every single day against Christians and Christian values everywhere in our country.

> OUR COUNTRY'S SECOND WAR IS HARDLY EVER TALKED ABOUT OR EVEN UNDERSTOOD.

This second war began much earlier than the first. It was after World War II that the moral standards that had bound our nation and our people together for generations first began a major turn to unravel. Said another way, that particular event set into motion forces that changed forever the way Americans work, play, build families, and conduct our lives as our government became the world's greatest superpower in these Last Days. Since World War II the moral values in our country have deteriorated more than in all of the previous years of our country's existence combined. Historians refer to this event as one of the greatest events in human history as it completely changed the course of history.

Earlier I read from the Gospel of John where Jesus said, referring to Satan, *"He was a **murderer** from the beginning, not holding to the truth. When he lies he speaks his native language, for he is a **liar** and the father of lies."* Today many in this enlightened age think it weird or downright silly to believe in a real devil. Jesus, however, identified Satan as a real, tough, formidable, and determined enemy.

In this particular verse, Jesus points out two key characteristics of Satan:

1. He is a liar.
2. He is a murderer.

Satan will use both methods to attack and attempt to overcome God's people. Throughout the history of the church, Christians have been subjected to both methods of attack. In Revelation 13, it is prophesied that in the Last Days of the church age, there will rise up a major superpower Satan will employ as a weapon to attack Christians and Christian values.

The history of mankind reveals Satan has always actively opposed any spiritual development originated by God. He is always on the attack, always trying to undermine and destroy God's purpose. God's

DECEPTION WAS ALSO AT THE VERY HEART OF SATAN'S SUCCESS.

spiritual enemy never remains idle. His tactics are consistently ruthless and deadly. He always plays hardball, and he never calls for a spiritual ceasefire! Spiritual warfare will always be the norm whenever and wherever God's light is shining.

Earlier, I discussed one of the primary strategies used by Satan since the very beginning of mankind—*lying or deception*. That is how he was able to convince Adam and Eve to disobey God's Word. Later, he caused lawlessness and wickedness to prevail in Noah's time until it became so terrible God would eventually decide to cleanse the whole Earth with a flood.

Deception was also at the very heart of Satan's success in developing a spirit of rebellion and permissiveness in ancient Israel and the root cause of spiritual failure among their leaders. Included in that list are a number of spiritual giants like Samson, King Saul, King David, and Solomon. By the time Jesus was born, most of Israel had descended so far into deception they could not recognize or accept Him as the true Messiah and God in the flesh.

Because the laws of our country were designed to protect our religious freedom, Satan's attacks against Christians in America have necessarily become more creative. Over the last forty to fifty years, his deceptions have rapidly destroyed many of the biblical moral standards the majority of Americans had lived by since the very founding of our nation.

WE ARE LIVING IN ENEMY TERRITORY.

During the past generation, spiritual deception has caused the **world's influence on Christians** to increase at a much greater rate than the **influence of Christians on the world**. Sins that first became permissible in American society just thirty or forty years ago are now largely acceptable to many Christians. Overtime, we have gradually become more tolerant of and apathetic toward the many sins that have become commonplace in our culture. Seemingly, the majority of Christians in America **no longer have a strong fear of sinning** or any of its consequences.

In this chapter, I am going to shift gears and take a look at the other primary strategy Satan uses against God's people. Because Satan is a murderer, this method includes persecution.

However, before I continue, I want to make a brief comment about a concern that may be bothering some of you: Why does God ever allow any deception or persecution of any of His people? At this point, I won't go into a deep discussion of this subject, but I do want you to keep a couple of things in mind.

First, we must always remember we are God's people, and as such we are living in enemy territory. Colossians 1:13 states, *"For he* [Jesus] *has rescued us from the dominion of darkness* [this world] *and brought us into the kingdom of the Son he loves."* Second, this world is not our home. The Bible says it is Satan's kingdom. That is why In Matthew 4:8–10 and Luke 4:5–8 Satan was able to offer this world to Jesus; however, Jesus turned him down. We are here as ambassadors of Christ—Christian soldiers—and yes, that does involve spiritual warfare.

I will illustrate persecution by reviewing a recent time in history. History provides many instructive examples of persecution. For our purpose, a review of only one will suffice.

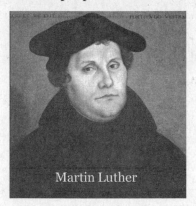

Martin Luther

Five hundred years ago, the Reformation had a profound, and very positive, effect upon the Christian world. Basically, it was a protest movement aimed at religious abuses. Those protestors birthed what we know today as *"pro-test-ant"* or Protestant churches.

Most historians would say the dominant figure in that particular movement was a German monk named Martin Luther. His nailing of the 95 Theses to the Castle Church door in Wittenberg on October 31, 1517, is seen as the spark that ignited the spiritual flames that blazed across Germany and the rest of Europe.

Now fast forward to 1933. It was a little more than four hundred years after the Reformation began. Again another leader had risen to national and international prominence in Germany—this time, on the political stage. His agenda was in stark contrast to Luther's. His name was Adolf Hitler.

Coinciding with his military aspirations, he was also passionate about his hatred of the Jews. Like a modern-day Haman, the man from the Bible story of Esther, Hitler didn't keep his feelings a secret.

As early as 1922 he had allegedly told a journalist: "Once I really am in power, my first and foremost task will be the annihilation of the Jews … I will have gallows built in row … Then the Jews will be hanged indiscriminately, and they will remain hanging until they stink … As soon as they have been untied, the next batch will be strung up … until the last Jew in Munich has been exterminated."

True to his ambition, almost immediately after coming to power, a series of laws were passed excluding Jews from various professions. Lawyers were disbarred; judges were dragged from their chambers and beaten up by Hitler's private army of hoodlums masquerading as storm troopers. Jewish students were forbidden to attend universities.

In 1935 German Jews had their citizenships taken away and they lost all of their civil rights. Think of it: One such individual was Albert Einstein, who was, at the time, in America. He later went to Belgium but never again returned to his native land. The orchestra conductor Bruno Walter fled after being told the hall where the Berlin Philharmonic performed would be burned down if he went through with a concert that had been scheduled there.

In his speech introducing this change in the laws, Hitler made it clear that if these measures didn't work, the problem would be handed over to the National Socialist Party for a (quote) "final solution." That expression—"The Final Solution to the Jewish Problem"—soon became code for the way Nazis viewed extermination.

Soon Hitler took control of the nation's newspapers, police, indus-
tries, courts, and schools. Then young children were taught to spy

for the Nazis, even on their parents. The majority of Germans
simply accepted these changes.
Those who did protest were
forced to leave the country,
imprisoned, or simply shot.

Hitler's Jewish agenda was
intensified in 1939 when his
elite troops took over Poland,
home to about two million Jewish people. After that all Jews were
restricted to ghettos where they were put to work in support of the
Nazi war machine. The Warsaw Ghetto was the largest, with a population of 380,000. Living conditions were horrendous, averaging 9.2
persons per room. Food was scarce, and many died of starvation.
There were occasional uprisings in the ghettos, but the fighters could
not match the superior German firepower: Therefore, they were
never a real threat.

Nazis then established
special extermination camps
where unsuspecting Jews
were taken on trains. The
Germans appointed groups
of Jews in the ghettos with
the gruesome task of deciding
which of their number should

be sent off next. We are talking here about very large numbers of
deportees being sent to who-knows-where, for who-knows-what.
We now know about the gas chambers, the overworked people who
wasted away due to starvation, and the awful medical experiments.

Back then most Jews were completely unaware. In the course of one 52-day period, 300,000 Jewish people from Warsaw alone were put on the dreaded trains and shipped to these ghastly evil places where they would eventually be put to death.

Community leaders who refused to cooperate with the Germans were shot in the head. One entire group chose to commit suicide rather than go along with what was happening.

BACK THEN GERMANY WAS A NATION OF HIGHLY EDUCATED AND CULTURED PEOPLE.

In 1941, when Germany invaded Russia, there were again several million Jews who lived in the newly conquered territories. This is when accounts of the death squads became relevant. Forced to lie down next to each other in large open pits, Jews were systematically shot by the Nazis. Immediately a second group of unfortunates were marched into the same pit and ordered to stretch out on the bloody bodies beneath them, where they too met the same fate. This process was repeated over and over until the giant hole was completely filled with bodies. Finally, the victims were covered over with a layer of dirt.

I think you get the picture so I won't go any further with this—I'll stop and try to make my point.

I do want you to hear me. Back then Germany was a nation of highly educated and cultured people. It still is. Germans, as a people, are among the most industrious. The population includes good bankers and fine musicians. It's the homeland of Bach and Beethoven. Germans are thrifty, dance a lot, and love their meat and beer. In many ways they're just like a lot of Americans (although many Americans are no longer very thrifty!).

How could it be that when Hitler came to power there were a

half-million Jews living in Germany, and when the war was over *all* but 30,000 had either fled the country or been killed?

I have tried to be straight forward and factual in what I have said. I haven't shown you any of the emotionally disturbing pictures that are widely available. I haven't related any of the heart-wrenching personal stories. I've not tried to make you feel nauseous, although that's how it can make one feel while researching this material.

I encourage you to look up "Holocaust" on the Internet. Just reading the material on Wikipedia (the Web's free encyclopedia) is worth your time. That way you can absorb this information at your own pace.

"But why even bring this up?" you may ask. "And in a Christian book!"

The answer is simple. These events relate directly to the message I am trying to present. They serve as an undeniable illustration of the conviction I have regarding the possibility of what some believers may go through in the days ahead.

Later I will explain in greater detail, but I would first like to state my heartfelt conviction in a single sentence.

The followers of Jesus Christ in America should guardedly prepare for the persecution of Christians. I'm not talking about another ethnic holocaust, but rather the possibility of a specific holocaust of the saints.

> "PERSECUTION," BUT IT NO LONGER SEEMS TO EVOKE A MEANINGFUL RESPONSE AMONG CHURCH PEOPLE.

I'm well aware that the word "holocaust" is practically owned by the Jews, and I can easily understand their intense feelings about it. What they experienced as a people seems unimaginable and awfully close to unforgivable. So to borrow their term without somehow seeking someone's permission feels a little like stealing. In the end, however, my apprehension gave way to a stronger desire to have you hear what I'm saying. I could have used the term "persecution," but it no longer seems to evoke a meaningful response among church people. Talking about Nero burning Christians as torches in the night—hundreds of them—to light the Roman roads, is so far removed from our everyday experience that it doesn't stir us like it should. It was too long ago and too far away. I needed a more current example, one that might stir the emotions as it can't be denied or dismissed.

> THERE WAS SOMETHING DEMONIC DRIVING THE PERPETRATORS.

I wanted you to feel the utter helplessness of these innocent people as they were being put through such unimaginable horrors for no reason other than a fact of birth: They were Jews. They weren't troublemakers. They were some of the most upstanding people in the entire German nation. Worse yet, they weren't even given the option of converting to another faith in order to escape their fate. They were singled out for extermination only because they were Jewish. I have to believe there was something demonic driving the perpetrators of this terrible crime against humanity.

The key passage of scripture in this book is Revelation 13. It describes a superpower that will emerge at the end of this present age and align itself with that liar and murderer Satan, and—here I quote from verse seven of this chapter—*"make war against the saints and … conquer them."*

Just as Hitler made war on the Jews, treating them mercilessly, the "beast" or superpower of Revelation 13 makes war on the saints. It doesn't take a whole lot of intuition to figure out whom Revelation 13 is talking about.

And, just as Hitler and his troops hated every Jew with a passion, so too Satan, in his alliance with the beast, fosters a climate of sharp anger and extreme bitterness toward the Christian community. It will become more vehement as these Last Days progress.

I realize some of you may interject, "But didn't you say in previous chapters that the beast could be what a backslidden America government is becoming? I don't see that Americans would ever allow something like what happened in Germany with the Jews."

I hope you're right, but my better sense tells me Christians need to seriously consider this possibility. Using a simple real life example, I'll show you why.

Ask yourself how Americans of the 1950s and 60s would have responded if told that by the year 2000, legal abortions would exceed 45 million in our country (that number is now well over 50 million); that praying aloud or discussing the Word of God in public schools would be prohibited; passing out condoms to middle-school and high-school students would be considered acceptable and practiced on a wide scale; more than fifty percent of marriages, involving both Christian and non-Christian couples, would end in divorce; crime would increase by five hundred percent; addiction to pornography even among Christians would reach epidemic levels; sexual immorality of all kinds would be rampant; greed and dishonest conduct would become the norm rather than the exception. Most of us, I believe, would have correctly expected an answer along these lines: "I find it hard to believe the American people would ever allow such things to happen."

Let me set before you a proposition. Consider the following: Both scripture and history tell us that spiritual warfare is real.

> SPIRITUAL WARFARE
> IS REAL.

Revelation chapter 12 states that after Jesus rose from the dead, Satan was hurled to the Earth and he is filled with fury. We are warned he furiously makes war against Christians. The history of the church over the last two thousand years confirms this truth. During this period of time, approximately 70 million Christians have been killed. It may surprise you to know that over 40 million of those killed, have been killed **since** the year 1900.

AMERICA HAS COME UNDER A VERY HEAVY SPIRITUAL ATTACK.

America was founded on Christian values. Except for Israel, God has intervened more in the spiritual development of our country than any other in history. As a result, **America has become the world's center of Christianity.** In these Last Days, Christians in America have a special calling from God.

We know from scripture that Satan has always devised schemes to corrupt and destroy anything God raises up. This truth is demonstrated over and over again in the Old Testament, as well as in the history of the church.

Two unique things have happened in our country during the last generation:

1. We became the greatest superpower in the history of mankind.
2. Even though there are now over 300,000 churches in America, our moral values have deteriorated more in this one generation than in all previous ones combined.

It should be clear to every modern-day believer that America has come under a very heavy spiritual attack. We were once known as a Christian nation, and the enemy is determined to make that title a thing of the past.

Given these events, wouldn't you agree we should at least consider how America matches up with the spiritual warfare prophecy of the Last Days? In Revelation 13 the Lord describes in great detail the superpower of our time. Our nation fits every descriptive characteristic of the beast/superpower. I will not review all of Revelation 13 in this book as I did verse one. I do that in my book *You Are Salt & Light*.

Revelation 13:7 states this beast/superpower was *"given power to make war against the saints and to conquer them."*

Then verses 9 and 10 state, *"He who has an ear, let him hear. If anyone is to go into captivity, into captivity he will go. If anyone is to be killed with the sword, with the sword he will be killed. This calls for patient endurance and faithfulness on the part of the saints."*

War is not fun like a video game. It is filled with real terror, beyond being terrible.

"Conquer" is not a pleasant word either. It means to subdue by force. Being subdued by force doesn't sound like something any of us would like.

These two words remind me a lot of the words Jesus spoke just days before His crucifixion during His Olivet Discourse. On this occasion, His disciples asked Him about signs related to His coming and the end of the age. This was His reply: *"Then you will be handed over to be persecuted and put to death, and you will be hated by all nations because of me. At that time many will turn away from the faith and will betray and hate each other"* (Matthew 24: 9–10).

At this point, it might be beneficial for you to review all of Matthew 24. I would like to quote a few more verses from this chapter about what Jesus had to say regarding the end of the age:

"For then there will be great distress, unequaled from the beginning of the world until now—and never to be equaled again.

"If those days had not been cut short, no one would survive, but for the sake of the elect those days will be shortened.

"At that time if anyone says to you, 'Look, here is the Christ!' or, 'There he is!' do not believe it.

"For false Christs and false prophets will appear and perform great signs and miracles to deceive even the elect—if that were possible. See, I have told you ahead of time" (Matthew 24:21–25).

Those words from Jesus about false prophets performing great signs make us aware of the fact that the diabolical plans of Satan and the beast/superpower include a very unique helper. It is described in Revelation 13 beginning with verse 11.

"Then I saw another beast, coming out of the earth. He had two horns like a lamb, but he spoke like a dragon.

"He exercised all the authority of the first beast on his behalf, and made the earth and its inhabitants worship the first beast, whose fatal wound had been healed.

"And he performed great and miraculous signs, even causing fire to come down from heaven to earth in full view of men.

"Because of the signs he was given power to do on behalf of the first beast, he deceived the inhabitants of the earth. He ordered them to set up an image in honor of the beast who was wounded by the sword and yet lived.

"He was given power to give breath to the image of the first beast, so that it could speak and cause all who refused to worship the image to be killed.

"He also forced everyone, small and great, rich and poor, free and slave, to receive a mark on his right hand or on his forehead, so that no one could buy or sell unless he had the mark, which is the name of the beast or the number of his name.

"This calls for wisdom. If anyone has insight, let him calculate the number of the beast, for it is man's number. His number is 666" (Revelation 13:11–18).

Bible scholars say this is the third member of an unholy trinity that includes Satan and the superpower beast, and they get a religious partner. The final participant has lamb-like qualities and supposedly performs supernatural acts. It directs people to worship, but in the wrong way. I discussed the religion of Humanism earlier that has become so dominant in our society and directs our worship towards *self*, though the majority of people are not aware of it. Me, myself, and I become the center or the driving motivational focus in most everything done. That is the very nature of Satan.

With the spirit of Humanism controlling the hearts of so many people, it is not difficult to realize why they would be open in allowing everything to be put under the control of the first beast by means of a mark—especially if an economic collapse occurred, and it was the only way you could buy or sell anything. Many economists state such a collapse is highly possible as our debt picture continues to sour and the value of the dollar declines.

In our modern world, this new mark could be as simple as a tiny computer chip inserted under the skin. Without it you would be unable to purchase groceries or gasoline, new clothing or fuel to heat your house in the winter. Being reduced to bartering or begging would be an enormous handicap, especially if survival is your number-one priority.

"But wait! Wait just a minute," someone interjects. "Won't the church be raptured before any of these events actually take place?" My reply to that is currently, there are several different views concerning the Rapture. I have my own, but at this moment that is not our concern. Obviously, first century Christians were not raptured, nor were any others down through the centuries. What about the Jews under Hitler or the many Christians being persecuted throughout the world as I write?

So, what does it mean right now to you and me if there is a "saints" holocaust or persecution of Christians in America? I believe we have to guardedly prepare for that eventuality. I'm picking up on the word "guardedly" from the text of the Olivet Discourse, where Jesus tells His disciples, **"You must be on your guard."** Christ's followers should guardedly prepare for the persecution of Christians.

I don't believe He meant for us to live in constant fear of an ill-fated tomorrow. On the other hand, neither did He mean for us to just ignore His warnings.

Rather, like the Jewish people have done, we should accustom ourselves to the realities of this world. More specifically, we must realize that just as anti-Semitism is an evil that must be guarded against, so there is also a latent anti-Christ-ism that we would be foolish to pretend does not exist. Jesus Himself said, *"You will be hated by all nations because of me."* In another similar statement He says: *"If the world hates you, keep in mind that it hated me first."* So far, the American church has not yet experienced a high degree of negative recharacterization relative to who we are and what we stand for, but the presence of this kind of opposition is becoming more apparent and more aggressive with each passing day.

> "IF THE WORLD HATES YOU, KEEP IN MIND THAT IT HATED ME FIRST."

Our Jewish friends, especially those living in Israel, live with a constant awareness that there are powerful forces out there, that even in this day and age, want to wipe them off the face of the earth, and surely would if they could. That's not an easy fear to live with, but it is a reality. Unfortunately, this same reality applies to Christians as well. The enemy of men's souls has every single believer in his sights. That's a fact of life. Every day his agenda is to do us great harm, and he's very good at it. To think otherwise is to be hopelessly naïve. If you recall I have discussed in this book some details how Satan has been very successful implementing his battle plans in our society through **decep-tion.** To *dismiss the thought* that this great spiritual battle might someday include physical persecution is only wishful thinking. Throughout history it has happened many times, and most likely it will occur in our

> THE ENEMY OF MEN'S SOULS HAS EVERY SINGLE BELIEVER IN HIS SIGHTS.

society at some point in the future. I think you can count on it.

As inconceivable as it may seem and in spite of the obvious fact that we are inhabitants of a very cultured and highly educated nation, as Jesus said, every follower of His needs to guardedly prepare for an intense attack by Satan through persecution.

SEVEN

—∽—

FAVORING OUR CHILDREN AND GRANDCHILDREN

If the present trend continues unchecked, the devil's hold on our society will soon turn into a death grip. For the faithful of this generation, serious intervention on behalf of our children and grandchildren is no longer optional.

It must have been an awful time to be alive compared to other generations—one of the very worst. You are probably scratching your head right now, trying to guess what I'm talking about. I'm not surprised! I would never have figured it out either.

I am referring to the time after Israel's twelve spies had finished exploring the land of Canaan; virtually everyone chose to identify with the majority report. In a nutshell, it said the place is just as wonderful as we were originally told, but the people are very powerful, and we'll never be able to defeat them. Numbers 13:33 states, *"We seemed like grasshoppers in our own eyes, and we looked the same to them."*

Here is Numbers chapter 14:1–4: *"That night all the people of the community raised their voices and wept aloud. All the Israelites grumbled against Moses and Aaron, and the whole assembly said to them, 'If only we had died in Egypt! Or in this desert! Why is the LORD bringing us to this land only to let us fall by the sword? Our wives and children will be taken as plunder. Wouldn't it be better for us to go back to Egypt?' And they said to each other, 'We should choose a leader and go back to Egypt.'"*

By this time the Lord had heard enough complaining, and He made an emphatic decree that everyone twenty years or older would never ever enter the good land He had sworn to make their home. The only exceptions were Joshua and Caleb, whose minority report simply said, "We should go for it!"

God speaks in Numbers 14:31 and 32, *"As for your children that you said would be taken as plunder, I will bring them in to enjoy the land you have rejected. But you—your bodies will fall in this desert."*

Could anything be worse than living out the rest of your life in the harsh environment of a desert with absolutely no prospect of a better existence? What an awful position to be in. This had to be a most discouraging situation knowing their future was, basically, just marking time until they died.

Trying to back track, the people then decided to make amends by going to war on their own, without God's blessings. It didn't work, and they were soundly defeated.

Then, instead of choosing to live their lives for the benefit of their children and grandchildren, their proverbial pattern of grumbling resumes. That's when we get the account about the rebellion of Korah found in Numbers 16:1–40. I'll pick up the ongoing narrative following that rebellion with Numbers 16: 41–50:

"The next day the whole Israelite community grumbled against Moses and Aaron. 'You have killed the LORD's people,' they said.

"But when the assembly gathered in opposition to Moses and Aaron and turned toward the Tent of Meeting, suddenly the cloud covered it and the glory of the LORD appeared. Then Moses and Aaron went to the front of the Tent of Meeting, and the Lord said to Moses, 'Get away from the assembly so I can put an end to them at once.' And they fell facedown.

"Then Moses said to Aaron, 'Take your censer and put incense in it, along with fire from the altar, and hurry to the assembly to make atonement for them. Wrath has come out from the LORD; the plague has started.' So Aaron did as Moses said, and ran into the midst of the assembly. The plague had already started among the people, but Aaron offered the incense and made atonement for them. He stood between the living and the dead, and the plague stopped. But 14,700 people died from the plague, in addition to those who had died because of Korah. Then Aaron returned to Moses at the entrance to the Tent of Meeting, for the plague had stopped."

This dramatic scene of a grey-haired, wrinkled old Aaron running in his priestly robes, censer in hand, to strategically position himself between the people and the plague is deeply moving as God's hand of judgment had already begun to fall.

These are the very same rebellious whiners who, time after time, had spoken out against both him and his brother Moses. In fact, these are the exact same men and women who got Aaron into trouble back in Exodus 32 when they insisted Moses took too long coming down from the mountain when he met with God. On that occasion, they talked Aaron into making them a golden calf like those they had learned to worship back in Egypt. What a disastrous series of events that was! Aaron undoubtedly learned from that mistake and knew he never wanted to make one like it again.

Now he was frantically trying to rescue them. There he was, all sweaty with censer or firepan in hand. Its flame had come directly from the sacred altar and had ignited the special incense that was used to make atonement for this generation of Israelites that seemed naturally inclined toward mutiny. Thousands had already died, but that was just a fraction of the huge number that would have perished had Aaron failed to act so quickly. The truth is, the surviving members of the entire adult population of Israel owed their very lives to this bearded old gentleman.

Later, in Numbers 20, Moses took his brother Aaron along with Aaron's son Eleazar, and climbed Mt. Hor. There Moses removed Aaron's priestly garments and put them on Eleazar. *"And Aaron died there on top of the mountain. Then Moses and Eleazar came down from the mountain, and when the whole community learned that Aaron had died, the entire house of Israel mourned for him thirty days"* (Numbers 20: 28–29).

THE ENGULFING POWER OF A HEAVEN-SENT REVIVAL

In earlier chapters I drew your attention to the identity of the frightening beast/superpower of Revelation 13, who at some future date will make life miserable for believers. Prophetic scripture supports the theory that this beast is our federal government during these Last Days as the people of America continue to backslide and abandon Christian standards.

I stated at the beginning of this chapter, if present trends continue unchecked, the devil's hold on our nation will become a death grip. Restated, in the absence of some incredibly powerful counterforce to challenge what the enemy is doing, his schemes will prevail and surrender is inevitable.

Is there any restraining element capable of doing just that? Yes, I believe there is! It is the engulfing power of a *heaven-sent revival* sweeping through the church and spilling over into the non-church world as well. That is why the faithful of this generation must take the task of intervening for our children and grandchildren more seriously.

Let me break apart this word, *revival*. In the middle is the root word *viv*. *Viv* words are all life-related. *Vivid* means "full of life." Someone who is *vivacious* is a lively person. *Viva!* is a call *"to life!"*

The *viv* in the middle of revival tells you that the word is about life. The prefix *re* means "again." So it's "again-life," or life coming back again. When a person has fainted, your hope is that he or she can be revived. In similar fashion, when the church, generally speaking, appears to have fainted, the thought is that it can be revived.

The suffix *al* means "pertaining to," so revival literally means "that which pertains to life coming back again" or "to live again." If housing starts are down, and construction and sales suddenly start moving again, there's been a revival in the housing market. In theatre, when an old play is dusted off and re-mounted, it's called a revival of that production.

In a special way, however, the word *revival* has always belonged first and foremost to the church. There it refers to a time when the people of God show evidence of a new way of living in the very presence of the Lord with incredibly powerful results.

Even the most awesome revival in the history of the American church, however, won't necessarily save this nation from her probable fate. I suspect the future history of America will be similar to the pattern of Israel as recorded in scripture. The start was on a high note, but the inspiration that accompanied that beginning is never really understood by following generations. Eventually, the author and underwriter of every blessing is forgotten and considered irrelevant to the national well-being. The majority of people got their eyes off of the one doing the blessing and onto what they were being blessed with. That began the general direction of a spiritual downward trend.

Even though there are intermittent periods of revival, or upward spikes, these never fully match earlier spiritual highs, and over time the bottom falls out.

"If this pattern is inevitable," you might ask, "then why get excited about promoting revival?"

In reply, I would contend that outstanding movements of God like these are capable of saving at least a generation or two. On a personal level, this is meaningful, because many of us have children and grandchildren or at least are acquainted with those who do.

> OUTSTANDING MOVEMENTS OF GOD LIKE THESE ARE CAPABLE OF SAVING AT LEAST A GENERATION OR TWO.

What revival actually looks like is my emphasis for this and the next two chapters of this book.

I hate to think about what the alternative will mean for America if we don't experience revival. If for whatever reason it doesn't happen, every Christian needs to ask, "Then what?" That concern is what prompted me to say, **the faithful of this generation need to take seriously their role to actively intervene for our children and grandchildren.**

To intervene is to come between or to interfere—to keep some otherwise-foregone conclusion from happening. It's to act in a precipitous manner, just as Aaron of old did.

It may well be that we are a generation that needs to abandon selfish thinking that says, "What about us, God? What do you mean we can't fully embrace all the good life has to offer? That's not fair!" Who can deny God has been gracious to our generation? The time has come for us to begin focusing on how we can help our precious children and grandchildren prepare for what could be an impending disaster.

I'm certain most contemporary Christians would much rather live in a time of revival than during a period of spiritual lethargy. It's no great honor, being on a playing field where the enemy is constantly running up the score against the church. Seeing what is going on in America, an objective observer would be hard-pressed to say the American church is influencing society anywhere near as much as society is influencing the church. Does this conclusion require more proof? I don't think so. More than enough has already been provided, and the case is closed.

Obviously, America is headed in the wrong direction, and what lies ahead is not good. The worst is yet to come. Listen to me … the legacy you leave for your children and grandchildren will have to be something of more value than someone who was always there when they played soccer, never missed a recital, or participated every year in the Grandparent's Day program. As admirable as these things are, they won't prepare your precious ones to stand for Jesus when virtually every peer is buying into the words and the powerful influence of the antichrist spirit as they find themselves completely surrounded by a society that has willingly embraced that same deceptive spirit.

"What do you want us to do?" you ask. Before I answer that question I want to first lay a foundation for what we can do.

AMERICA IS HEADED IN THE WRONG DIRECTION.

Great industrial companies often hire people with specialized skills to handle emergency breakdowns whenever they occur. As a group, these employees are trained to quickly restore order wherever interruptions occur. These individuals have a unique passion to identify and correct problems. Coming from a lifelong career in the corporate business world, I understand this concept very well.

In the Kingdom of God things are not much different. The primary mission of God's people is to be the salt of the earth and the light of the world. When a moral breakdown occurs—a decline in the spiritual health of the nation or the church—our spiritual DNA causes us to become deeply concerned.

Every Christian is free to labor quietly as long as the spiritual life of the church and the country are not threatened. However, when things begin to go astray from the path of truth, and you witness a moral decline like we have experienced during this past genera-

tion, then *we who are truly committed to the Lord's work must be willing to spring into action in an open, fearless, and perhaps even a way some might call fanatical.* The dire circumstances of the times demand it. If we stand by and do nothing, we risk losing all of God's blessings, including His hedge of protection. Should that actually come to pass, it will be because His people did not care enough or love the Lord enough to actively advocate and defend His standards.

> BE WILLING TO
> SPRING INTO ACTION.

Combating the decline of moral standards in our nation should be a high priority ministry of the church. Unfortunately, many are not tuned-in to the problem or its consequences. No longer can the conventional work of the church be our main focus. **We must deal with the breakdown at hand,** as we alone possess the solution to this problem. Dealing with it is our responsibility. It cannot be the responsibility of the people in the world. In fact, the majority do not realize how serious the problem has become for our country. Like it or not, we are God's soldiers in a spiritual struggle for the very survival of godliness in America.

God's Word has given us a framework for national revival. In 2 Chronicles 7:14 He says: *"If my people, who are called by my name, will humble themselves and pray and seek my face and turn from their wicked ways, then I will hear from heaven and forgive their sins and will heal their land."*

I think it is ironic the Lord spoke these words to Solomon during a time of great prosperity, much like America has experienced throughout the last generation. I think we should take particular notice of the fact that God sets specific conditions for revival by starting this discourse to Solomon with the word "if." He then proceeds to list four "ifs" that must be satisfied by God's people prior to His promise of a response. The first "if" requires them to *humble themselves*, the second is *prayer*, the third directs them to *seek His face*, and the fourth is to *turn from their wicked ways*.

Revival is what it will take to preserve true biblical Christian standards in our country, not only for our benefit but also for our children and grandchildren. It is a responsibility that rightly falls directly on the shoulders of God's people. If we are indeed willing to replicate God's established framework for national revival, the Lord will surely restore the Christian heritage of our country and safeguard it for the next generation or two.

Revival, although closely linked with evangelism, should not be confused with evangelism. Revival is an experience, while evangelism is more

REVIVAL IS WHAT IT WILL TAKE.

of an expression. Revival is a fresh demonstration of God's power. In these days of acute political ineptness, moral lawlessness, and spiritual weakness, we desperately need a revival powerful enough to stop and ultimately reverse the hellish wave of statistical evidence that has completely engulfed an entire generation.

I firmly believe God wants to prepare His people for a great earthly offensive against militant godlessness, not only within our secular society, but also within the political arena. Sometimes godlessness is even found wearing the deceptive mask of religion. One of the main objectives of this book is to prepare you for such a revival and the attendant outpouring of the Holy Spirit.

Let me suggest a few possibilities that might explain why we have not already witnessed such a revival:

1. It could be related to the fact that the Christian message has become so highly commercialized. Too many who proclaim the message use nearly every tactic possible to get the tithes of widows and the poor, while at the same time, they indulge themselves in luxury living and shamelessly beg for more!

2. We have allowed the gospel to be cheapened. We can never quit preaching that the cross of Jesus Christ coupled with spiritual re-birth is the one and only path to Heaven. Acts 4:12 states, *"Salvation is found in no one else, for there in no other name under heaven given to men by which we must be saved."*

3. Individual carelessness. Perhaps we spend too little time in prayer and lack a dedicated commitment to expand the Kingdom of God.

4. We too often fear what others may think or say. Instead of using every opportunity to proclaim the only name whereby all men must be saved, we allow intimidation to rule over us and effectively silence any prompting of the Holy Spirit.

5. Our prayers lack urgency. This may very well be the biggest single factor contributing to the delay of a Holy Spirit-led revival.

6. Perhaps we have acquired a taste for the glory that belongs to God and to Him only. Jesus said, *"I do not accept praise from men"* (John 5:41) and *"How can you believe if you accept praise from one another, yet make no effort to obtain the praise that comes from the only God?"* (John 5:44)

Now back to the question of what actions you should take. At this particular time, **I'm suggesting four companion steps** to go along with the four outlined in 2 Chronicles 7:14. A couple of others will be added before you finish this book.

I'm fully aware each step will require some serious thought and time on your part. In fact, the truth is, when you've completed everything I'm recommending, you will still find it necessary to regularly reassess and revise your conclusions.

Step number 1, however, could and should be finished immediately. I sincerely hope you will give it a try. Here it is:

STEP 1: Create a *circle of love* and fill in the names.

A *Circle of Love* is simply a listing of those people who mean the most to you. Older Christians could include many names in their *circle*. For example, if you were married and had several children, who in turn gave you grandchildren and, subsequently, great-grandchildren, the number in your *circle* might reach into the thirties, forties, fifties, or even higher. My wife and I presently have seventy-six in our immediate family, and it is still growing.

If you don't have great-grandchildren yet, it's more likely your total, including children, their spouses, and some grandchildren, will range between ten to thirty people. That's still a lot of people.

Couples with younger children probably won't break into double digits. Then again, you might want to include parents and siblings in your *circle of love*.

Singles can put down quite a few names as well. Nothing limits your *circle* to blood relatives alone. If you enjoy a close relationship with a friend or neighbor, that individual should definitely be included. After all, it is *your* *circle of love*.

STEP 2: Carefully think through what you can offer each of these special individuals that might be of eternal value.

It could be lessons learned from a lifetime of living for and trying to follow Jesus. But, for whatever reason, these insights have never been shared with a son, a daughter, or close friend: Now you're feeling divinely compelled to do just that.

Possibly it's a special book or an experience that totally turned your life around, but those close to you know little about it.

Maybe it's the promise of Grandpa's persistent prayers or the phone calls to find out how they're being answered. It could be the money needed to send a grandchild to a Christian school, or a short-term mission trip with Mom before your daughter heads off to college, or simply sharing the story of how you became a follower of Jesus. You always put it off in the past, but now you feel the need to write down your testimony including how the Lord brought you through some really difficult times. It's whatever the Holy Spirit lays on your heart as you think about each of the precious individuals on your list. This is what I have to share with my son, or my closest friend, or my granddaughter, that I believe has eternal value. You might say to your fiancé, "It's my life verse, sweetheart, and believe me, I've said it to myself time and again! And because we're going to be married, I wanted you to know about it."

STEP 3: For each person in your circle of love, write down specific prayer requests applicable to the present, as well as five or ten years into the future.

At this very moment, what should I be requesting of the Lord that will benefit Emily? Too often our prayers are hasty and shortsighted. "Lord keep Emily healthy, pretty, and sweet!" That's not adequate. Instead how about:

"Lord, protect her from the evil one. Give her teachers at school and church who will love her and challenge her to be a special servant for You.

"Five years from now, Lord, I want You to be the one who guides her as she considers if she should plan on going to college, as well as which one to attend.

"Ten years off—start preparing her for a single life of celibacy, if that's how she can best serve You, or choose the right young man to join her in marriage."

When you finally stop long enough to write down each request and regularly make an effort to update your list, I think you will be surprised to find many prayers of hope have somehow been replaced with prayers of expectation.

"Lord, maybe my forty-three year-old son-in-law needs to make a career change. He's making good money, but he has almost no time for church or family. Please give him wisdom regarding his career path."

"Dear Jesus, my wife is a true saint. But I think she gives so much of herself, that she gets depleted. Help me know how to either teach her to sometimes say no, or help fill her tank in some way that I'm not aware of."

"Heavenly Father, I fear my son lacks a certain spiritual toughness. I ask You to help me think of ways to provide that for him."

Finally, to the best of your ability, write down the specifics of how you want to pray for each of these individuals. Only as you do this will you be transformed into a prayer warrior strong enough to stand between your loved ones and the plague of the enemy that now permeates our entire culture.

To *intercede* is to go to God on behalf of another. Unlike spiritual superficiality, effective intercession requires serious forethought. Anything less will not suffice. Given the times we live in, it should not be difficult for any believer to grasp its importance.

STEP 4: Examine your own life. What changes is God asking you to make?

Today in America the devil is winning. In my heart I can hear the wake-up trumpet playing *Reveille*. Reveille—revival—same basic idea … wake up! And what does that mean for me, Lord? "I certainly don't want to be found lolling around watching a 50" LED TV while the emergency siren is sounding in the street!"

In a safe harbor setting for all kinds of seductive distractions, ongoing self-examination is important. If you hope to be an effective disciple of the Son of God, it is crucial.

As I close this chapter, I once again would like to review the four steps of my action plan.

They are:

1. **Fill in the names on your *circle of love*.** I would do that today.
2. **Think through what you have to give each of these special individuals that has eternal value.** That will take a while, but you should begin the process now.
3. **To the best of your ability, write down your request for each of them beginning with the present and continuing to five and then ten years into their future.**
4. **Examine your own life. What changes is God asking you to make?**

Also, as I conclude this chapter, I don't want to sound overly dramatic, but I can somewhat identify with Moses of old whose senses were immediately attuned to imminent danger whenever it was in the air. Face down on the ground with his brother Aaron, he knew that God's warning meant there wasn't a whole lot of time left before bodies would begin dropping.

"Take your censer and put incense in it, along with fire from the altar," he literally commanded Aaron, *"and hurry"* (as if, I can't do the job God assigned to you), *"hurry to the assembly to make atonement for them."*

That very nearly describes the way I feel as I put down these words. You must listen. I cannot do your job. If you don't provide cover for your loved ones, no one else will, and they could perish. This threat is real. You can't ignore the powerful influence Satan has gained through our society. People are going to be lost if you fail to intervene on their behalf. The time to begin this process is right now. There is no more time left to waste, so "get a move on" and "hurry up."

> IF YOU DON'T PROVIDE COVER FOR YOUR LOVED ONES, NO ONE ELSE WILL.

Hey—I told you before that adventures often involve real danger. This is not an exercise in make-believe. What we are experiencing is both hazardous and exciting. Perhaps now you are starting to believe me. That certainly is my prayer!

EIGHT

SENSING THE LORD'S PRESENCE

Momentum is a highly valued commodity in many competitive enterprises. In the world of sports, it's good to be on a roll—every team member is in sync. Confidence level peaks, and everyone on or off the bench senses that their team is almost unstoppable. Championships are won or lost depending on which side captures the momentum at a crucial point.

The world of politics is very similar. Candidates for public office want their campaigns to peak at just the right time. It's important for a wave of momentum to accompany their effort immediately before voters cast their ballots.

Similarly, when wars are fought, momentum becomes important. In Ken Burns' captivating fifteen hour documentary series about World War II, we are reminded that in the beginning of that global conflict the Axis powers possessed all the momentum. In Europe, the Nazi blitzkrieg had proven unstoppable as Germany marched into Poland and later France. The same was true of Japan's lightning conquests in the Far East.

If General Tojo had chosen to focus on Southeast Asia, instead of attacking America's naval base in Hawaii, he probably would have captured access to every resource he desired without provoking an all-out war with America. And if Hitler had completed the conquest of England before engaging his troops with Russia, the outcome in that theatre of conflict would no doubt have been dramatically different. In hindsight it is obvious that these ill-conceived decisions led to a negative shift in the momentum their troops had enjoyed and, eventually, the annihilation of both war machines.

In spiritual warfare, momentum is once again an important factor. Only those who don't have a clue about what is actually going on in America would deny that it is Satan who has captured virtually all of the momentum in recent decades. This shift has occurred not because the U.S. church has become impotent, but, rather, because overtime it has lost the societal clout it once enjoyed. Earlier chapters highlighted the nature of this deterioration and the alarming extent of our enemy Satan's aggressive moves.

TURNING THINGS AROUND IN AMERICA DEPENDS ON AUTHENTIC REVIVAL.

At this point, I truly believe turning things around in America depends on authentic revival—one that is totally inspired by and led by the Holy Spirit. Unfortunately, that term doesn't impact present-day Christians in the same powerful and positive way familiar to previous generations of believers. Too often people today will tend to associate "revival" with pictures of sweaty-faced preachers who holler a lot, sawdust-trail evangelism, and even backwoods snake-handlers.

Beginning in this chapter I am going to approach the term "revival" from a somewhat different angle. Taking time, at this point, to examine it more carefully seems to line-up appropriately with my contention that another overwhelming move of God's Spirit through the churches of this land is the only real hope for an outcome quite different than what most churches have been experiencing.

Do you like the idea of experiencing a stronger presence of the Lord? It is my guess this would have a good sound to almost everyone.

The most outstanding characteristic of genuine revival through-out history is an overwhelming sense of the Lord's presence. Revival, above all else, is a purposeful glorification of the Lord Jesus Christ. It is a restoration of Him as a living personality to the center of life in the Church. During every period of revival, you will find with-out exception, there has always been a tremendous increase in the emphasis upon His actual personhood and the unique power of the blood He willingly shed on Calvary.

Just imagine what it might be like if Jesus began attending your church on a regular basis. Picture the difference it would make, and you will have a pretty good idea of what revival in your church would look like.

In my example, say Jesus attends your church in bodily form for a month or even two. Now I know that every Sunday He is with us in Spirit, but what if He were physically present and you could see Him, not just through eyes of faith but with your own two eyes? What difference would that make?

PURPOSEFUL GLORIFICATION OF THE LORD JESUS CHRIST

Following is a list of responses, seven in total, I think you might very well observe. By design, it does not cover every base because I have reserved a key one for later discussion. It does, however, give you a good feel for what would take place.

ONE: If Jesus were to bodily join in your church service, I believe your first response would be immediate *worship*. As soon as someone recognized Him ... people would begin to nudge one another and whisper, "Is that who I think it is?"

Then I would expect the room to become very quiet. Next, some would probably go over and humbly bow before Him, maybe even quietly prostrating themselves on the floor. The term worship means to attribute worth to God—to praise or adore Him. These acts are the body language of worship.

Someone might begin to sing, "Jesus, I adore You. Lay my life before You. How I love You!" I can hear the praise music continuing, uninterrupted, for quite some time.

Would you believe renewed worship is actually one of the early signs of revival in a church? It is an expression of people trying to honor their Lord and Savior, because they want to fully acknowledge what He means to them.

TWO: Love. Were Jesus to come to your church Sunday after Sunday, it wouldn't be long before the people would start to extend Christ-like love to one another. Knowing this was extremely important to Him, they would do their best not to act in a way contrary to His desires. Negative feelings toward someone would be put on hold, at least for a little while. Why? Because our Lord is right there with them in His church, and this issue is one He has repeatedly emphasized.

I don't know if you are aware of this, but remarkable evidences of love between congregation members always characterize times of revival. "It was like we were living in liquid love," is a comment that came out of revivals in western Canada from several decades back. Other participants said, "We were extremely careful with our words, because none of us wanted to be responsible for ruining what was being experienced."

THREE: With Jesus present in bodily form, many would want to talk to Him. You can easily imagine a long line of folks waiting patiently for their turn.

Maybe some people would only say, "Thank You, Jesus." It's also quite possible they would have a personal request, or they would want to talk to Jesus about a loved one. Some would ask for forgiveness. Others might declare, "I love You," or "You're wonderful."

Prayer, or talking to Jesus, and revival go together hand in glove. You never, ever find revival without extra ordinary times of prayer. Times of persistent and prevailing prayer are always one of the key factors leading to revival.

FOUR: *God's Word begins to come alive* for people during periods of authentic revival. This doesn't mean Jesus will be doing the preaching. Look at it this way: If I am standing behind the pulpit and Jesus was sitting with the congregation, you would constantly be looking in His direction for some evidence of approval. And if He says amen to something I say, it will underscore my words in an incredibly powerful way.

It is fair to report that in times of revival, the scriptures possess an amazing power to convict. Hearers don't question what is said. Instead, they willingly submit to the authority of the Bible.

FIVE: When men and women perceive that the Lord is near, they are unusually anxious to *serve*. They might very well say, "You've done so much for me, Jesus. What can I do to show my gratitude?" The gifts they have received from God are now offered back to Him. No one says, "I'm sorry, I can't," "I'm too busy," or "It's not a good time for me right now." Instead, the church has such an abundance of volunteers, it's almost as if an apology is in order. "Check back again in a couple of weeks, and we'll see what new ministries are beginning that might need some help," becomes a standard reply.

SIX: When Christians sense that Jesus is there, numerous friends and acquaintances begin to accompany them to church. "You just have to meet Him," they tell others. "He'll change your life. I mean, there's no one quite like Him in the whole world." *Evangelism* is no longer seen as some kind of burden or some obligation. Rather, it now becomes the very lifeblood of every individual whose life has been made new because of a personal encounter with their Savior.

SEVEN: This one may or may not surprise you. The presence of Christ also provokes an immediate response from the enemy. In fact, intense *spiritual warfare* is actually precipitated by the advent of revival. As soon as new life begins to emerge, the enemy does everything within his power to abort it. He begins by exploiting every weakness of the church leaders, then attacks the flock with a determined vengeance, concentrating first on those who are spiritually feeble. He goes after the most spiritually feeble in the flock in whatever way he can. That's just the way he operates. His ruthlessness knows no bounds.

So revivals can be "crazy." The great London preacher Charles Spurgeon called them "seasons of glorious disorder." Times of revival aren't exactly Heaven on earth, even though it does provide us with a taste of what it will be like. At the same time, however, the forces of darkness will spare no effort to squelch any momentum as quickly as possible.

As you consider these seven signs of revival in the local church, try to evaluate where your church stands in relationship to each of these evidences. Here they are again:

1. An increased and intense participation in *worship*
2. An outpouring of *love* for one another
3. A growing boldness in every aspect of *prayer*
4. The preaching and hearing of *God's Word* as anointed by the Holy Spirit
5. An eager renewal of interest in all outlets of Christian *service*
6. A remarkable sense of confidence and eagerness in *evangelism*
7. A display of both wisdom and maturity when *spiritual warfare* begins

Hopefully, you now have a more complete picture of what

happens to a church when the presence of Jesus becomes a reality for every member. Personally, I find these characteristics attractive. I think you will, too. I would certainly hope so, because all revivals are intended to be high-water marks in the life of a church.

Revivals possess an innate power to bring glory to the Lord, as well as to inflict a defeat on the

REVIVALS POSSESS AN INNATE POWER TO BRING GLORY TO THE LORD.

enemy. In a book published several years ago, Arthur Wallis presented a word picture demonstrating the force of revivals. The name of the book, appropriately enough, is *In the Day of Thy Power*. Following is a direct quote:

> *"There was once an ancient reservoir in the hills that supplied a village community with water. It was fed by a mountain stream, and the overflow from the reservoir continued down the stream bed to the valley below. There was nothing at all remarkable about this stream. It flowed on its quiet way without even disturbing the boulders that lay in its path or the foot-bridges that crossed it at various points. It seldom overflowed its steep banks, or gave villagers any trouble. One day, however, some large cracks appeared in one of the walls of the old reservoir, and soon afterwards the wall collapsed, and the waters burst forth down the hillside. They rooted up great trees; they carried along boulders like playthings; they destroyed houses and bridges and all that lay in their path. The stream bed could not now contain the volume of water, which therefore flowed over the countryside, even inundating distant dwellings. What had before been ignored or taken for granted now became an object of awe and wonder and fear.*

From far and near people who in the usual way never went near the stream, hastened to see this great sight."

Wallis continues:

"In picture language this is revival; in fact it is the sort of picture language that scripture uses to convey the irresistible power of God. Often in the period just preceding the movement, the stream of power and blessing has been unusually low. The people of God and the work of God have been 'in great affliction and reproach,' despised or ignored by those around them. In response, however, to the prayers of a burdened remnant God has been quietly heaping the flood. The watchful eye has seen 'a cloud as small as a man's hand.' The listening ear has caught 'the sound of abundance of rain.' Then suddenly, when the majority had no expectation of it, God opened the windows of heaven and poured out the blessing so that in the channels of organized Christianity there was not room enough to receive it. … Stubborn wills that have long withstood the overtures of the gospel, the pleadings and the prayers of loved ones, now bend and break before the irresistible flow of the Spirit, to be engulfed themselves and borne along in the stream of blessing."

I realize this is rather a long quote, but it uniquely underscores a key point. My conviction: There is no doubt a powerful revival is the only hope we have of foiling Satan's plan for our land. Unless the church in America soon experiences another extended season of coming-to-new-life-and-vigor, I'm afraid our cause is all but lost.

Here is a point that is important to understand. The message of revival is for the church. It is impossible to *re*-vive something that was never alive. Genuine revival within the church is characteristically accompanied by many conversions. Revival sermons, however, shouldn't be confused with evangelistic sermons.

The old-time revival preachers in America were fond of claiming it made no sense to preach to non-Christians about new life in Christ when the church was not even close to what it should be. New converts attending church for the first time in their lives would be forced to conclude that the message, in real life, doesn't actually work. On the

HOW DO YOU EVALUATE THE CHURCH IN AMERICA?

other hand, when baby believers became part of a renewed congregation, there was every reason to believe they would continue to mature in their faith.

How do you evaluate the church in America? I'm not talking about a specific congregation because, praise the Lord, there are always good examples. In this context, I am referring to the North American church in general. Is it going about its business in the same way it would if Jesus Himself were sitting in a pew Sunday after Sunday?

I don't think so.

One of the saddest pictures in the entire book of Revelation is found in Chapter 3. It is here our Lord evaluates the church in Laodicea. It is the last one on a list of seven churches He talks about, located in the territory we know today as Turkey. It is somewhat like the picture I described earlier. Jesus Himself shows up unexpectedly, and this is what He tells them:

"You say, 'I am rich; I have acquired wealth and do not need a thing.' But you do not realize that you are wretched, pitiful, poor, blind and naked."

Those are awful words. You are wretched, or contemptible; pitiful—pathetic, lamentable; poor—needy, lacking in what has true value; blind—without the basic ability to see what's going on; naked—not clothed, exposed!

"I counsel you to buy from me gold refined in the fire, so you can become rich; and white clothes to wear, so you can cover your shameful nakedness; and salve to put on your eyes, so you can see."

These are straightforward words. You don't have to wonder what they mean.

"Those whom I love I rebuke and discipline," He says next. *"So be earnest, and repent."*

To say it another way, He is demanding a significant change in their behavior.

What follows are some rather strange words addressed to this particular church—not from the pulpit, but from somewhere outside the building. Again, Jesus speaks directly to a specific congregation.

"I stand at the door and knock. If anyone hears my voice and opens the door, I will come in and eat with him, and he with me."

This is a most unusual picture. The Lord is standing *outside* the building, knocking on the door imploring someone—anyone—to come and let Him in. Once it is opened, He promises the warmth of His presence will permeate and transform the entire assembly.

These words of our Lord were spoken to a specific New Testament congregation located in the city of Laodicea. I believe they are entirely applicable to many congregations in present-day America. He is saying: "If you are wondering where I am, I'm outside knocking on the door waiting to be invited in, bringing with me new life for all. Through eyes of faith, you will be able to see me participating with you in everything that's going on. Is that something you want?"

Life coming back again with momentum—the life of Jesus Himself once again is powerfully manifested throughout in the church. Does that sound appealing to you?

I ask because revival is the only force powerful enough to stem the present tide of evil. We need to talk openly and often about spiritual revival in the church, the right place to start so that we can begin to recapture the momentum the church has lost.

WE NEED TO TALK OPENLY AND OFTEN ABOUT SPIRITUAL REVIVAL IN THE CHURCH.

Earlier, I mentioned seven key responses to the presence of Jesus that I would expect if He were in attendance in your church. These seven characteristics were included in the description of authentic revival given by people who had experienced it in their own church. At this point, I want to introduce an eighth and final characteristic that was purposely left out of my original list. It is the concept of personal revival—what it looks like and how to experience it.

Using the same word picture of Jesus being physically present in the church, I want you to get a feel for what revival in a home might look like. How would having Jesus as a houseguest affect the way you live? It would most certainly put everyone on their best behavior. Try to imagine two siblings engaged in a loud argument and a concerned parent, putting a finger to their lips and forcefully whispering "Shhh!" while, at the same time, anxiously pointing upstairs to remind them that Jesus is in their house.

Would family members actually work at being as polite as possible to one another? Would put-downs be kept to a minimum and affirming words spoken more often and more consistently?

Certainly family crises would be handled differently with Jesus in the house. His very presence would foster a much greater sense of peace and security. Jesus preached that a house built on the Rock could survive any and all storms that beat against it.

Anyone fortunate enough to be honored with the visit of such a wonderful guest would want every friend and associate to meet Him. Times would be scheduled for countless social occasions where others could learn what it's really like to be so very close to the most important person who ever lived.

It's conceivable, and most likely, personal attitudes would be scrutinized. With penetrating honesty, Jesus might authoritatively challenge someone's use of time or money. Should that happen too frequently, an uneasy feeling might begin to hover over the arrangement. Sooner or later some might become so offended they would find themselves suggesting, "For the sake of everyone involved, Jesus, we think maybe You would be happier living somewhere else."

In reality, people aren't usually that up-front when talking with the Lord. They are much more likely to simply start ignoring Him—acting as though He is not even there—and rationalizing their desire to send Him packing. "He deserves something better—something more suitable for a king, a safer environment."

How wonderful it is when a Christian finally realizes Jesus is, in fact, an unseen guest in their earthly home. His presence is far more precious than expensive furniture in the living room or a swimming pool in the back yard. This privilege is not just wishful thinking; it is an absolute truth that is central to the very definition of personal revival.

To understand personal revival, you must fully embrace the concept of living with Jesus as your constant companion. Doing so will make you aware of His closeness.

Personal revival can be identified by an ongoing sense of the presence of the Lord. Just as a church experiences the presence of Jesus during revival, so also, do individuals. What I am describing is a heightened awareness of holiness.

Even those who are considered spiritual leaders can become very uncomfortable when fully exposed to the holiness of God—Isaiah 6 is a powerful and illuminating passage about a great prophet who loved the

> **PERSONAL REVIVAL CAN BE IDENTIFIED BY AN ONGOING SENSE OF THE PRESENCE OF THE LORD.**

Lord deeply. Upon seeing God sitting on a throne high and exalted, and hearing the seraphs crying out to one another, *"Holy, holy, holy is the LORD Almighty,"* Isaiah found himself in a most dreadful situation and cried out: *"Woe to me! ... I am ruined! For I am a man of unclean lips, and I live among a people of unclean lips, and my eyes have seen the King, the Lord Almighty"* (Isaiah 6:5).

How offensive the society in which we live must be to God. Consider just for a moment, how you might feel standing in His holy presence as a representative of this culture, knowing full well what is displayed each day—via movies, television, magazines, the internet, books, and other media outlets—along with the results of a study claiming that the Lord's name is used in vain over *one billion* times each day. How could anything be more shameful, more so in America than other countries, because of our Christian heritage and the fact the Bible is so readily available and open to everyone? Does it shame you enough, with what is happening in our society, to join with others in an honest effort to save Christian values and halt the onslaught of rampant evil in our society?

Because revival is characterized by an overwhelming sense of the presence of a holy God, it naturally follows that conviction of sin, confession, and even reconciliation, are typical events for any-one affected. For revival to be long-lasting, however, the real task is to not only break the old negative patterns, but to firmly establish new positive ones in their place.

The apostle Paul wrote about taking off old clothes and putting on clean, fresh ones. Remember how wonderful it feels when you first try on a new outfit. Revival arrives with the same sense of expectations, only it's the putting-on of sparkling-clean spiritual clothing.

> PERSONAL REVIVAL RESULTS IN A SENSE OF GREAT INWARD JOY FOR THE PERSON EXPERIENCING IT.

Tears are often present during times of personal revival. They usually accompany the softening of a heart made ready to receive God's forgiveness. Experiencing anew the clean sensation of God's holiness, we begin to feel more fully alive than ever before. In short, I want you to understand that personal revival results in a sense of great inward joy for the person experiencing it.

Is there a specific sin standing between you and what I'm describing?

Usually people who are really serious can accurately identify what they have been holding on to that needs to be abandoned before a meaningful change can take place.

The bottom line is this: Sin and the presence of Jesus don't mix. They never have and they never will. You have to choose one or the other.

Those who regularly sense the presence of Christ, which comes with personal revival, are immediately convicted when they find themselves acting in a manner that has been unrighteous. They are brutally honest with themselves, which brings a quick response to ask the Lord for forgiveness and anyone else who might be affected. Personal revival is quite effective in highlighting the continuing importance to walk righteously. It is a time of new beginnings, of new life, of dedicated revival.

At this time you certainly would be right in asking me, "What about you Bob Fraley—have you experienced personal revival?"

For me, the dramatic encounter I had with the Lord in June of 1971 during which He identified the beast/superpower of Revelation 13 was the beginning of personal revival in my life. Why it happened at this time, I am not sure. However, I have always felt it was because **I believed this Word from the Lord**, even though at the time there was no evidence of this being the proper interpretation on Revelation 13. I still recall exactly how I felt as the Spirit of the Lord fell on me—flooding my heart with the presence of Jesus. This event is so permanently etched in my memory that even now, after more than forty years, it is still as clear as though it took place yesterday. It is not that I wasn't serving the Lord at the time. I was involved in church leadership and teaching the adult Bible class. However, it marked the beginning of a new life for me, walking with faith that I had heard from the Lord, along with a holy fear that inspired obedience to whatever the Lord called me to do.

> YOU TOO CAN
> EXPERIENCE
> PERSONAL REVIVAL.

How personal revival dramatically changed my life and that of our family I share in the recent book, *The Blessings of Obedience*. It covers several experiences of our walking with the Lord during the last forty years. (See the details of how you can receive a *free copy* of *The Blessings of Obedience* at the end of this book.)

You too can experience personal revival. However, only the Lord can make it happen. Reach out to Him in prayerful conversation. Let Him know the desire of your heart—how much you want it. Be persistent! He will not disappoint you.

NINE

—∞—

NATIONAL REVIVAL:
THE URGENCY OF THE TIMES

The window of opportunity for national revival will not remain open indefinitely. When Jesus entered the city of Jerusalem the people were shouting "Hosanna." "Hosanna" means "Save us now!" We desperately need to discover that same urgency.

America is at a crossroads. Will we choose revival or judgment by the hand of a Holy God? I choose revival! How about you?

I think just about everyone would agree life can't be lived in a constant state of urgency. In our present-day world, many live as though it is absolutely imperative that many things be done right now, when the truth is, it probably wouldn't make much difference if they put it off until tomorrow—or even next week, for that matter.

I am not saying there can't ever be an issue that demands prompt attention. I think anyone hearing a police loudspeaker sounding a call to evacuate their house immediately because a wildfire was rapidly approaching their neighborhood, would be wise to clear out as fast as possible. That would be a situation that definitely warrants an urgent response.

My topic for this chapter fits somewhere in between these two examples. It's not something that has to be acted upon this very moment. Then again, neither is it a matter that should be neglected for very long. It does require attention, and it should be addressed sooner rather than later.

My subject for this chapter is **national revival**. Just as individual believers need to experience personal revival and the presence of Jesus in a powerful new way, individual churches need to experience revival and an overwhelming sense of the presence of the Lord. History proves that sometimes entire countries find themselves impacted by God manifesting Himself in a unique way when this happens.

> CHANGE IN THE DIRECTION ON A NATIONAL LEVEL TAKES PLACE.

You get glimpses of this latter miracle occurring in ancient Israel. Numerous times in the Old Testament, there are accounts of such times. Does everyone repent and turn back to the Lord? Of course not! However, generally speaking, a change in the direction on a national level takes place because a significant number of inhabitants are able to get things straightened out with the Lord.

In the past, believe it or not, America has experienced the same kind of transformation. Later in this chapter, I will tell you about one such time out of several times of spiritual revival in America.

Earlier, to make a point, I referred to a rapidly moving fire. If you were warned that one was approaching your neighborhood, it would be prudent to react quickly. Many people mistakenly believe all wildfires can be controlled. Firefighting experts insist that this isn't true. Some fires can't be stopped until they burn themselves out. Others cannot be controlled at all.

For example, in 1967, the Tasmanian fires in Australia came on the heels of a considerable drought. More than 110 known fires were burning on the morning of February 7, consuming more than 650,000 acres in about five hours.

American preachers of earlier generations had a much better feel than we do for what a revival can accomplish. They struggled, however, to come up with a vivid picture that would adequately convey the phenomenal power of a revival. The image they turned to most often was a sweeping wildfire blown by the winds of the Spirit and burning everything in its path. As sparks of a wild-fire from one area that's ablaze are carried by the wind to ignite somewhere else, so it is with revival. The stories of what has been happening in a given church are told elsewhere, and interest in the spreading of a Spirit-led revival grows.

I am convinced the time is now for pastors across the country to begin calling for a revival with a new sense of urgency—one that will sweep across the nation. We desperately need the imme-diate intervention of a spiritual force so overwhelming it would be impossible to harness—in part because so many fires would all be burning at the same time—110 in the Phoenix area, 110 in the Chicago area, another 110 around Atlanta, 110 more near L.A., and at least 110 around New York and Philadelphia, Boston and Washing-ton, D.C. In fact, I envision flash points touching down in towns, large and small, all across America.

THIS COUNTRY FACES THE RISK OF A TERRIBLE JUDGMENT AT THE HANDS OF A HOLY GOD.

For this kind of wildfire to begin and spread, churches everywhere must be convinced this rising tide of power—of national revival—is America's only hope. The church has to be confident that God is both willing and able to do something amazing and blazing in our day. If He could bring Nineveh to her knees through the preaching of one reluctant prophet, what might happen in our time if there were many will-ing servants of the Lord eager to minister on His behalf?

Christians need to fully understand that absent another great revival, this country faces the risk of a terrible judgment at the hands of a holy God. Dr. Billy Graham, Dr. Henry Blackaby, James Robison, Pat Robertson, Bill McCartney, the late Bill Bright, and David Wilkerson, along with many other prominent Christian leaders, have expressed a fear that America is racing toward God's judgment. Rapid deterioration in moral values continues in America and, as I said before, nothing—neither new programs, education, counseling, nor anything else—seems to have a significant effect on the problem. It seems to worsen with every passing day.

> CHOOSE YOUR FIRE—
> EITHER REVIVAL
> OR JUDGMENT.

Since the beginning of mankind, God has never allowed any nation to embrace sin to the degree now seen in America and remain exempt from punishment. This is especially true when the people had the Word of God available to them as we do. The Bible warns us that we shall be held accountable for how we make use of the resources and opportunities God has given us. We need to take Luke 12:48 seriously. I am going to repeat what it says:

"From everyone who has been given much, much will be demanded; and from the one who has been entrusted with much, much more will be asked."

In other words, American citizens can't live as though they will never have to pay a price for evil behavior. Even Israel, God's chosen people, did not get a pass on that.

The ancient warning of the prophet Amos is appropriate for our day as well. He said, *"Seek the LORD and live, or he will sweep through the house of Joseph like a fire; it will devour, and Bethel will have no one to quench it"* (Amos 5:6). It's as though this man of God was saying, "Choose your fire—either revival or judgment." Even if a backslidden America is the beast/superpower in Revelation 13, those same two options are the only ones available from which we must choose. In fact, it just may be that government officials opposing Christian standards will one day gain so much control they will become a tool of God's judgment. As most of us can see, this is already beginning to happen. Could God be warning us?

However, for the sake of the Christian community, our children, and grandchildren, I will do all that I can to see that the believers of this generation say, "We choose revival."

But we must sense the urgency of the times. Our window of opportunity won't remain open forever—we need to respond while God is still calling. We don't have unlimited options or any way of knowing how long they might last. We would do well to learn from what happened in Noah's day. Those people obviously waited too long. Will we?

OUR WINDOW OF OPPORTUNITY WON'T REMAIN OPEN FOREVER.

We humans don't have as much control of things as we often would like to believe. Even in the matter of conversion, a person is to respond when God calls. Said differently, the Lord is under no obligation to show up at our convenience. We should not realistically expect the great ruler of the universe to jump whenever we snap our fingers.

That's why nonbelievers are encouraged to say "yes" to Jesus before they leave an evangelistic outreach event or a church service. God has drawn so close to them, it seems as though He is whispering their name in an audible voice. "Not now," the person thinks, "I'll pray on my own when I get home." More often than not, it never happens. People should be informed that when the Lord prompts them, the Holy Spirit is drawing them, and they should respond immediately. The Lord may not draw them unto

Himself again. He is not our servant. Instead, we are to serve Him. He is the master. This is one of the first lessons every Christian must learn and acknowledge. We are to answer whenever He calls, not the other way around.

AN ENTIRE NATION CAN SIN AWAY ITS DAY OF GRACE.

Regarding the matter of national revival, there will undoubtedly come a time when God is no longer sympathetic to the cries of His people. Listen to these words of the prophet Jeremiah regarding Israel: *"Then the LORD said to me: 'Even if Moses and Samuel were to stand before me, my heart would not go out to this people. Send them away from my presence!'"* (Jeremiah 15:1)

The very same sobering concept is again expressed in Ezekiel 14: 12–14: *"The word of the LORD came to me: 'Son of man, if a country sins against me by being unfaithful and I stretch out my hand against it to cut off its food supply and send famine upon it and kill its men and their animals, even if these three men—Noah, Daniel and Job—were in it, they could save only themselves by their righteousness, declares the Sovereign Lord.'"*

Clearly an entire nation can sin away its day of grace, just as an individual can. America is edging closer and closer to such a time.

The window of opportunity for national revival will not remain open indefinitely. Consequently, we need to develop a sense of urgency—the power found in "Hosanna"—"Save us now!"

That was the cry of the people in the city of Jerusalem as Christ rode in seated on a donkey. Had He been riding on a stallion, it would have meant He was coming as a warrior! According to John, that is exactly what He does ride in Revelation 19: 11–16:

"I saw heaven standing open and there before me was a white horse, whose rider is called Faithful and True. With justice he judges and makes

war. His eyes are like blazing fire, and on his head are many crowns. He has a name written on him that no one knows but he himself. He is dressed in a robe dipped in blood, and his name is the Word of God. The armies of heaven were following him, riding on white horses and dressed in fine linen, white and clean. Out of his mouth comes a sharp sword with which to strike down the nations. He will rule them with an iron scepter. He treads the winepress of the fury of the wrath of God Almighty. On his robe and on his thigh he has this name written:

KING OF KINGS AND LORD OF LORDS."

On Palm Sunday, Jesus rode a donkey—still considered a noble animal in that day. To the people of that time, it meant He was coming in peace.

"Hosanna!" or "Save us now!" was the yell of a jubilant crowd as they spread palm branches and their cloaks before Him. "Hosanna

DISCOVER THE URGENCY OF "HOSANNA" – "SAVE US NOW!"

to the Son of David," they screamed. "Blessed is he who comes in the name of the Lord. This is the opportune time, Jesus. We believe you are the long-awaited Messiah. Save us now!"

And Jesus did. He definitely responded to their cry of "Save us now!" … but not in the way they had expected.

Even so, their sense of urgency needs to be recreated in our day. Jesus, we need you to act now! Show us your mighty power. Send us another national Spirit-operated revival. Now, as then, our most urgent need is still, "Hosanna! Save us now!"

I hope you are able to fully comprehend what I mean by saying that "the window of opportunity for national revival will not remain open indefinitely." Consequently, it is imperative that we, like the Jewish people who watched Jesus ride a donkey into Jerusalem, discover the urgency of "Hosanna" – "Save us now!" I want to use American history to show you exactly what that looks like in practical terms.

The effects of a powerful revival usually last only a generation or two. What happens is when people draw near to the Lord during revival, He blesses them in numerous ways. Unfortunately, their children soon begin to take this wonderful inheritance for granted. Ultimately, they prize the many benefits more than the One providing them. Complacency sets in and their hearts start to grow cold to the things of the Lord. Sadly, this story is typical and oft-repeated.

To give you a specific example, beginning in the 1730s and lasting at least a generation, America experienced a remarkable period of history known as the Great Awakening. By the early 1790s, however, the religious scene was totally different. Spiritual decline had once again set in.

After years of deprivation and struggle, suffering from the Revolutionary War had taken its toll. It is not uncommon for the fighting and killing of war to have a negative effect on the morals of the people involved.

Infidelity, imported from our military ally France, had swept across our nation, even infecting the lives of a number of influential individuals. They even had the audacity to deny the very existence of God, who ever so recently had been incredibly gracious in preserving America during the "Great Awakening" revival, influencing the basic principles set down in our Constitution.

In colleges all across the land, infidel clubs were organized with the express purpose of destroying what they had labeled the Christian "superstition." In the western frontier, which at that time consisted of states like Ohio, Kentucky and Tennessee, lawlessness ruled.

Deplorable moral conditions, coupled with the falling-away of many churches, prompted twenty three New England clergy to circulate a letter calling on their congregants to pray for revival. Their request was straight forward and to the point, saying let there be "public prayer and praise, accompanied with such instruction from God's Word, as might be judged proper, on every first Tuesday of the four quarters of the year, beginning with the first Tuesday of January 1795 at two o'clock in the afternoon … and so continue, from quarter to quarter, and from year to year, until, the good providence of God prospering our efforts, we shall obtain the blessing for which we pray."

> **CHRISTIANS WERE MEETING ONCE A MONTH FOR ALL-DAY PRAYER FOR REVIVAL.**

The response was overwhelming. In fact, all across the country, everyday believers entered into "covenants" to spend an entire day in prayer—I especially want you to pay attention to this—once a month. Christians were meeting once a month for all-day prayer for revival. There can be little doubt *they* were sensing the urgency of the situation!

Many also pledged to spend a half-hour every Saturday night, plus another thirty minutes every Sunday morning before church praying for revival. Can you picture this happening now?

Church members formed Aaron and Hur Societies to hold up the hands of their pastors. You may be wondering what Aaron and Hur had to do with this spiritual warfare taking place. The answer is found in the Old Testament, where a special incident of warfare involved Aaron and Hur in a unique way. Exodus 17:8–16 says:

"The Amalekites came and attacked the Israelites at Rephidim. Moses said to Joshua, 'Choose some of our men and go out to fight the Amalekites. Tomorrow I will stand on top of the hill with the staff of God in my hands.'

"So Joshua fought the Amalekites as Moses had ordered, and Moses, Aaron and Hur went to the top of the hill. As long as Moses held up his hands, the Israelites were winning, but whenever he lowered his hands, the Amalekites were winning.

"When Moses' hands grew tired, they took a stone and put it under him and he sat on it. Aaron and Hur held his hands up—one on one side, one on the other—so that his hands remained steady till sunset. So Joshua overcame the Amalekite army with the sword.

"Then the Lord said to Moses, 'Write this on a scroll as something to be remembered and make sure that Joshua hears it, because I will completely erase the memory of the Amalekites from under heaven.'

"Moses built an altar and called it The Lord is my Banner. He said, 'For hands were lifted up to the throne of the Lord. The Lord will be at war against the Amalekites from generation to generation.'"

I believe the last part of this passage relates to *the spirit* of the Amalekites, or the ways of the world, which Christians are still at war with today.

Another important influence growing out of these prayer meetings of the late 1700s came about as seminary students began to meet regularly to study the histories of revival. How, when, and why had God shown His powerful hand in days past? They sought detailed answers to these questions.

Given the expressed urgency of believers throughout the country, it wasn't long before fire from heaven began to fall. What has been called America's Second Great Awakening was characterized by three C's—colleges, camp meetings, and churches. Space doesn't allow me to do much more than cite a few relevant illustrations.

Colleges: Yale, for example, became a hotbed of unbelief and criticism of the Bible. Providentially, who should be made the new president of Yale in 1795 but the grandson of Jonathan

Edwards, a man who had been one of the key figures in the Great Awakening some fifty years earlier.

His name was Timothy Dwight, and the students gave him a list of lecture topics designed to make him sweat. The one he chose first was "Is the Bible the Word of God?" He then announced he would preach a chapel series in which he would respond to each of their negative arguments. His powerful messages soon began to change things on campus. In 1802, revival hit in full force when seventy-five in a student body of 230 (or about one in three) were soundly convicted. Of that seventy-five, nearly half later entered the ministry.

Camp Meetings: Imagine a large outdoor space with people constantly arriving on horseback or in covered wagons. That is what a camp meeting was like in those days. Following is a description of what you might have seen. There was no public-address system, so several services were going on at the same time. When people responded to a sermon, they didn't go up front or into an inquiry room. Instead, they actually entered an area formed by a variety of ministers holding hands to create what they called a "sacred circle." Inside that circle, those who came forward would kneel and pray, being under deep conviction by the Holy Spirit.

Here's how a Presbyterian minister described what he observed:

"A memorable meeting was held at Cane Ridge in August 1801. The roads were crowded with wagons, carriages, horses, and footmen moving to the solemn camp. Between twenty and thirty thousand persons were assembled. Four or five preachers spoke at the same time in different parts of the encampment without confusion. The Methodist and Baptist preachers aided in the work, and all appeared cordially united with it. The salvation of sinners was the one object. We all engaged in singing the same songs, all united in prayer, all preached the same gospel. The numbers converted will be known only in eternity.

"Many things transpired in the meeting, which were so much like miracles that they had the same effect as miracles on unbelievers. By them many were convinced that Jesus was the Christ, and were persuaded to submit to Him. This meeting continued six or seven days and nights, and would have continued longer, but food for such a multitude failed. To this meeting many had come from Ohio and other distant parts. These returned home and diffused the same spirit in their respective neighborhoods, and similar results followed. So low had religion sunk, and such carelessness had prevailed everywhere, I had thought that nothing common could have arrested and held the attention of the people."

Churches: There were no outstanding personalities to whom everyone looked and no one assuming the role George Whitefield had played in the first Great Awakening. Instead, pastor after pastor in church after church wrote exciting reports about the working of the Holy Spirit in the lives of their flock.

For example, in 1798 one minister reported his feelings prior to the breakthrough this way: *"No fond parent ever watched the fever of his child at the hour of its crisis with more anxious and interested feelings than numbers of God's praying friends watched the work of the Spirit at this critical moment. The thought of it going off were more dreadful than the grave."*

Now that's urgency!

This pastor's concerns were rewarded. The meeting house was filled service after service, and it was just a few days before he counted more than sixty converts.

The window of opportunity for national revival will not remain open indefinitely. Consequently, we need to discover the urgency of "Hosanna"—"Save us now!"

If Jesus were to attend your church service in bodily form, and you could call Him up for a short interview, how do you think He would answer the following question? Jesus, on a scale of one to ten, ten being an intense sense of urgency regarding the need for national revival, where would You place the average American Christian?

What do you think the Son of God would say?

What if you asked Him the same question regarding the average member of *your* church congregation? On a scale of one to ten, ten being an intense sense of urgency regarding the need for national revival, Jesus, where would You place the average member of my church?

WHAT WOULD HIS ANSWER REVEAL ABOUT THE FUTURE OF AMERICA?

How might He respond if you asked Him to tell you privately where He would place you as an individual on that same scale regarding an intense sense of urgency about the need for national revival?

What would His answer reveal about the future of America and of our children and grandchildren?

Because the window of opportunity for national revival won't remain open indefinitely, I am going to ask you to seriously consider the following challenge.

Are you willing to assume the role of a modern-day "Aaron and Hur"—to start praying for your pastor, your church, and our country? It doesn't matter if you pray alone or with a partner. Starting this week, **I want you to begin praying earnestly, with a sense of urgency,** for revival in the church where you attend, as well as every other church across the land. Set aside just fifteen minutes at least once during the week. This can be done at any time during the week. But continue your commitment of fifteen minutes per week for ten consecutive weeks.

You are to pray for your church, your pastor (or pastors), and anyone else the Lord lays on your heart, as well as every other

Christian church in America. Ask for a Spirit-led revival. Include praying for the Lord to honor us with a season of His presence.

You don't have to make up your mind immediately. If you say yes, however, the ten weeks should begin immediately. If you say yes a week from now, your ten weeks will begin then. Of course, you can re-commit for another ten weeks when your first ten weeks come to an end. I hope you will. Where I have had an opportunity to personally share this prayer request, I have been blessed with the response, as more often than not several would commit to pray for revival more often than once a week.

Let me also suggest you write down your commitment and post it on your refrigerator or that place where you post your reminders. In our busy world, it's not uncommon for any of us to forget things. Especially in those areas of spiritual importance as the enemy is always going to be at work, using any means he can, to side track us in any commitment we make to God.

WE MUST BE PERSISTENT AND STICK WITH IT.

Daniel had to pray for twenty-one days and not stop until he obtained his answer. We learn from Daniel 10:11–14 that we must be persistent and stick with it. We cannot pray for a thing once, then cease, and call that prayer the prayer of faith. Daniel's answer did not come for *twenty-one days* because the Bible says an archangel with the message was hindered by the devil.

Realize this commitment to pray is a start, and though small, it could be much more significant than most of us are able to comprehend. It could even be the impetus for a renewed sense of urgency marking a clear declaration of who we are and what we truly want God to accomplish through us!

How long must the Christian community pray for a

Spirit-led-revival before it happens? Obviously, I don't know! I do believe the devil will strongly resist, so we must be persistent and persevere.

—⚏—

TEN

WHAT WE HOPE FOR IS COMING ... DON'T MISS IT

In this chapter you will discover:

- **What Heaven is like**
- **What Hell is like**
- **How you can be certain you will go to Heaven**

"On the first day of the week, very early in the morning, the women took the spices they had prepared and went to the tomb. They found the stone rolled away from the tomb, but when they entered, they did not find the body of the Lord Jesus. While they were wondering about this, suddenly two men in clothes that gleamed like lightning stood beside them. In their fright the women bowed down with their faces to the ground, but the men said to them, 'Why do you look for the living among the dead? **He is not here; he has risen!** (emphasis added) *Remember how he told you, while he was still with you in Galilee: "The Son of Man must be delivered into the hands of sinful men, be crucified and on the third day be raised again."' Then they remembered his words"* (Luke 24:1–8).

In my mind, the word that best describes how the followers of Jesus must have felt after His crucifixion is "disheartened."

To me, it means to take the very heart out of someone, to weaken their spirit, to remove their courage.

"Dis" as a prefix makes a word its opposite. So "courage" becomes "discourage." "Hearten," which is really a great word, ends up as "dishearten."

The next day was all black for the friends of Jesus. Scripture records almost nothing about what took place in their lives, but we do know what His enemies were doing. They stayed busy. The end of Matthew 27 reads: *"The next day ... the chief priests and the Pharisees went to Pilate. 'Sir,' they said, 'we remember that while he was still alive that deceiver said, "After three days I will rise again." So give the order for the tomb to be made secure until the third day. Otherwise, his disciples may come and steal the body and tell the people that he has been raised from the dead. This last deception will be worse than the first.'*

"HE IS RISEN!"

"'Take a guard,' Pilate answered. 'Go, make the tomb as secure as you know how.' So they went and made the tomb secure by putting a seal on the stone and posting the guard" (Matthew 27: 62–66).

Stealing the body was probably the last thing in the world the disciples had in mind. What good would that do? Their world had just been shattered. They had no desire to prop it up with a lie. Without their leader, they were nothing more than a scattered group of former disciples who had just had their hearts ripped out.

Three words would soon change everything. Three short words—spoken by *"two men in clothes that gleamed like lightning."* This phrase is taken directly from the Bible (Luke 24:4). The text doesn't say so, but it seems obvious to me these men were angels. They didn't speak these words to the disciples, but rather to the women who came early on Sunday morning with burial spices for the dead body of Jesus. Those three powerful words were *"He is risen!"*

"Dear ladies, Jesus isn't here. Why look for the living among the dead? He is risen!"

The power of these three words alone would immediately transform a disheartening situation, accompanied by total despair, into
an occasion for great joy and excitement. Remove the "dis-" prefix.
Let "disheartening" once again be that delightful word "heartening."
"Discouragement" now reverts to "encouragement," or the infusing
of courage.

Potent words often possess the ability to totally change the
way people think!

When Jesus was crucified, the spirit of every disciple was completely crushed. The success Satan has enjoyed throughout our country in recent years, combined with the knowledge that a backslidden
America matches the prophetic description of the beast/superpower
found in Revelation 13, is both discouraging and disheartening.

From a tactical standpoint, this pattern is not new. Our spiritual
enemy has used it in the past. Satan's plans have always included
fierce warfare and the destruction of anything God has raised up.
Beginning with Adam and Eve, it permeates the history of God's
people throughout the entire Bible. It continued, unabated, throughout the two-thousand-year history of Israel, and the subsequent two-
thousand-year history of the church. Now that America has become
the nerve center of Christianity in these Last Days, it has become a
reality here.

I am a very patriotic person. I love America and agonize over
the continuing decay of moral standards in our country. Our
world is deathly ill. The hurt and pain resulting from the almost
constant spiritual defeats many Christians have suffered in recent
years is, at times, gut-wrenching. On a personal level, it hurts
that much! Moral values continue to deteriorate and it seems as
though nothing is able to put an end to the problem.

That perception, alone, is disheartening and discouraging.
Likewise, the revelation I received from the Lord in June of 1971

identifying the beast of Revelation 13 was both disheartening and discouraging. I felt trapped. I suspect Moses felt much the same when he found himself sandwiched between the army of Pharaoh and the Red Sea. There seemed to be nowhere to escape. His only choice was to look up. When he did, defeat was turned into victory and three million Israelites were delivered from a life of perpetual servitude.

THIS WAS MY "RED SEA" MOMENT.

This is somewhat how I felt after receiving this revelation about the "beast," and the Holy Spirit so strongly confirming the authenticity of this revelation in my heart. Up until this time, decision-making had always been a hands-on process in my life in which I had been fairly successful. This was different! This was my "Red Sea" moment, the one when I, too, would discover there is never, ever more than one choice. Because of it, my wife and I learned this one choice was to walk in obedience with the Lord by faith in holy fear. That has been the reason for our success for the saving of our family.

This is the final chapter of this book—lengthy compared to the others. I want to finish with a positive note of encouragement. That is my focus for this chapter. Those same three words of powerful declaration, *"He is risen!"* have the same meaning and impact today as they did when first spoken. These words can soften the feeling of disheartenment or discouragement you may experience as you contemplate what is happening in our country. With that said, I want us to explore: WHAT WE HOPE FOR IS COMING.

A poll of the American people taken by Market Facts Telenation on behalf of *US News & World Report* appeared in the June 20, 1997, edition of USA TODAY. It stated that sixty-seven percent of the adults polled are certain there is a Heaven. Additionally, it reported that **eighty-eight percent of these same adults who believe Heaven is real are certain that they are going to Heaven.**

Why do you think so many want to believe they will be going to Heaven? Is their belief based on a measure of certainty or merely something they hope is true? The obvious finality of this matter makes it difficult for most to accept the premise that they might not be going to Heaven. Down deep they know **there is only one of two possibilities:** It could very well be Hell! Either way, it is for eternity.

In this chapter, I am going to share some thoughts about Heaven, as well as Hell. You may agree or disagree with any of my comments. Either position is certainly valid. I have researched the subject extensively and truly believe my findings will bless and encourage you. Since I have not been to either place, my description will be incomplete and necessarily limited to the result of my research. However, I do think the descriptive phrases I share are in harmony with what the Bible has to say about each destination. Furthermore, you must understand it is virtually impossible for any human being to accurately describe either of these two places using human language. I am convinced Heaven is so wonderful, and Hell is so horrible, that no human mind is capable of fully comprehending either place.

> IT IS THE LORD'S DESIRE THAT EVERY HUMAN BEING SHARE HEAVEN WITH HIM.

It is the Lord's desire that every human being share Heaven with Him. Let me quote you just a few of the several verses found in the Bible that confirm this:

- *"God our Savior, who **wants all men to be saved** and to come to a knowledge of the truth. For there is one God and one* *mediator between God and men, the man Christ Jesus, who gave himself as* **a ransom for all men...** (I Timothy 2:3–5, emphasis added).

- *"For God so loved the world that he gave his one and only Son that whoever believes in him shall not perish but have eternal life"* (John 3:16).
- *"The Lord is not slow in keeping his promise, as some understand slowness. He is patient with you,* **not wanting anyone to perish, but everyone** *to come to repentance"* (2 Peter 3:9, emphasis added).

> THE SALVATION OF ONE SOUL IS WORTH MORE THAN THE COMBINED VALUE OF ALL THE THINGS IN THE WORLD.

The Bible was written and preserved to show us the very clear and sure way to Heaven. I certainly don't want to see anyone miss Heaven. I would never have devoted thousands of hours in teaching and writing if I had in any way doubted its importance. None of it has been done for financial gain. I do not take any monetary compensation for anything I write or for any of the time I spend teaching. Not because it is wrong to do so, but rather, because the Lord has provided my needs and those of my family through secular employment.

I will say this as boldly as I can: You definitely do not want to *miss* Heaven. After all, Jesus placed a greater value on going to Heaven than on gaining the whole world. He, better than anyone, could attest to how important it is. He said, *"What good will it be for a man if he gains the whole world, yet forfeits his soul?"* (Matthew 16:26)

The salvation of one soul is worth more than the combined value of all the things in the world. The choice is ours. We must choose between Heaven and Hell. It is an individual decision each of us must make before departing this Earth. Heaven is a free gift from God, but it is not without some conditions. The conditions are clear and simple. In fact, they are so simple most people want to gloss right over them. My earnest desire is to help you understand how very simple it really is and why choosing Heaven over Hell is undoubtedly the most important decision you will ever make in your entire life.

Before explaining to you how simple it is to know for sure that you are going to Heaven, I want to share with you a few interesting facts about both Heaven and Hell.

INTERESTING FACTS ABOUT HEAVEN

In the Bible the words "Heaven," "heavens," and "heavenly" occur 729 times—434 times in The Old Testament and 295 times in the New Testament. For most people, this word identifies the wonderful place where God centers His presence, where His throne is, where the holy angels reside, where the "many mansions" are located, and where the redeemed of the Lord will live in sinless joy forever.

Heaven is a spiritual dwelling place for our spiritual bodies, not a material dwelling place for our physical bodies. However, at present we can only attempt to identify and define Heaven using our physical senses. That is why the limited amount of descriptive words and phrases the Bible gives us about Heaven are of a material nature. In it we are encouraged to see Heaven as a totally unique place of immeasurable value with streets of gold, inhabitants living in beautiful mansions, and beautiful park-like surroundings. Familiar terms like these are used to convey a measure of value earthy minds can quickly relate to.

Over the years, a number of individuals have claimed the Lord showed them what Heaven is like. I believe some of these firsthand accounts offer valid enlightenment and are worth passing on.

The Bible says that a tree is known by its fruit. Therefore, I have only included the accounts of selected individuals, carefully considering how the Lord used each of them in the years following what they said were visions of Heaven.

For example, John Bunyan was on his way to an act of committing suicide when the Lord provided him with some wonderful insights of what Heaven was like. Afterwards, he was so inspired by the realities of Heaven, he wrote *The Pilgrim's Progress,* a book that has provided mankind with some much-needed direction to the land of realities.

After the Lord allowed him to witness the perfect and glorious utopia of Heaven, which he described as "exceeding by far the loftiest flights of human imagination," General William Booth became the human instrument used by God to found the great charitable work of the Salvation Army, an organization that still enjoys nearly universal respect.

Actually, over the last two thousand years of the church's history, hundreds of individuals in all stages of spiritual development having many different origins, speaking many different languages, separated in time by decades or, in some instances, even centuries, have claimed to have been the recipients of divine insights regarding Heaven. Even more amazing is the fact that among those whose fruits seem to confirm this possibility, there has been **perfect agreement with respect to hundreds of details even though they had never before communicated with one another**. If the source of these were not of divine origin, most of us would expect this unanimous agreement to be somewhat more elusive, if not totally impossible. If they were not from God, reporting different views of many countless details would be inevitable.

"No eye has seen, no ear has heard, no mind has conceived what God has prepared for those who love him—but God has revealed it to us by his spirit..." (I Corinthians 2:9–10). There are a number of

insights regarding Heaven that are worthwhile and deserve consideration, though it is hard for us to fully grasp what life in a purely spiritual realm would be like.

In Heaven humans will experience utter holiness. Jude 24 states we will be presented *"before his glorious presence without fault and with great joy."* We will reign with Christ in victory throughout all the ages. No words can adequately describe our mental state in Heaven. It will be so superior to anything we have experienced here on Earth. We will live in a continuous state of ecstatic joy so intense the nervous system here on Earth could not support or maintain such happiness.

> NO WORDS CAN ADEQUATELY DESCRIBE OUR MENTAL STATE IN HEAVEN.

In Heaven, every man is immortal. Our individual capacities are unlimited and supernatural. Our minds and motivations are completely void of sin. Our energy is boundless. This truly adds up to joy unspeakable, full of glory. The years never age us. We never again experience hunger or thirst any more. God wipes away every tear from our eyes—and we never again will experience any pain, fear, doubt, defeat, regret, misunderstanding, sorrow, or temptation. Our cup literally runs over.

There is no sickness, no pain, no suffering either physical or emotional, and no stress. Everyone lives, surrounded by beauty, in an atmosphere of complete peace and love. Every need is provided for. The very same loving God who created all of mankind is now caring for all those who truly love Him.

This environment will never change. Even though we cannot comprehend it, this new reality will last forever—for eternity. Everyone in Heaven lives a life full of joy, peace, love, and happiness. It will never come to an end.

John Bunyan reported that when he was caught up into Heaven, he had conversations with Elijah, Moses, and other Old Testament saints. General Booth stated he saw many patriarchs, many apostles of ancient times, and several of the holy martyrs, as well as an army of warriors who had fallen in every part of the world. These two men described Heaven as a place whose splendor is so magnificent the language of man cannot adequately convey it.

John Bunyan described many different thoughts the prophet Elijah shared during their conversations. One was the tremendous happiness that exists for everyone living in Heaven. Elijah described this atmosphere as a complete state of happiness. The body and soul are completely free and no longer affected by sin. In our world, every human being is familiar with the burden of sin in the world and in our flesh. It is heavy and weighs us down. In Heaven we will finally be free of it. Like a bird freed from life-long captivity in a cage, we will be free at last.

Everyone in Heaven receives a perfect spiritual body; the imperfect bodies we used here on Earth will be discarded. Everyone who has loved the Lord, from the days of Adam and Eve to the present time, will now call this beautiful, wonderful place home. We will each be equipped with a perfect spiritual body in which all can enjoy blessings that far exceed anything ever imagined here on Earth.

After experiencing visions of Heaven and seeing the state of saved man, General Booth attempted to describe the heavenly body, though he declared that it was impossible. In trying to do so, he stated that all disease and all the corroding work of the ages—the physical blemishes resulting from man's fallen state here on Earth—are done away with in Heaven. Booth said that to describe the shape and features of saints in Heaven was simply not possible, as they are, at the same time, both earthly and celestial.

It is beyond words to fully describe from what great depths God has exalted man to such superb heights in Heaven. On Earth, man is weak and sinful, but in Heaven we will appear with grandeur and beauty. We have complete assurance and faith that this is and will be the state of all those who trust in Jesus Christ for salvation.

The same grandeur attributed to the spiritual body of mankind in Heaven, has also been attributed to the living conditions. For example, people tell of the indescribable beauty found in every amazing thing of Paradise, and in each of the wonderful mansions. Words failed those who tried to compare the beauty and magnificence of the mansions provided for the saints to anything found on Earth. Even the palaces of nobility were judged to be inferior. Furthermore, the surrounding conditions in Paradise were seen as fully equal and no less impressive.

Although the words "gold" and "diamonds" are used in the Bible to imply extraordinary value, they even fail to adequately portray either the magnificence or the beauty of the surroundings that await all of God's people.

Every new arrival will be surrounded by a glory so dazzling and over-whelming, their capacity for enjoyment will be maxed out. Indeed, their cup will runneth over.

Because all of Heaven is a spiritual realm, everything in it is spiritual, and everything has spiritual value. The parks, the beauty that surrounds each edifice, the animals, the trees, the flowers, the lakes, the rivers, the crystal pools, the shape and size of the mansions, the gems, the jewels—everything contained therein.

Man will be perfected in Heaven. In the beginning, God made human beings in His likeness. The angels who attend, the angels who instruct, the music, the songs, the saints themselves (mainly in fellowship), the degree and manifestation of glory, light, and life— these and everything else in each park or palace are working harmoniously to promote the complete happiness and joy of God's people.

Together, they all contribute to the spiritual well-being and development of every saint who dwells there. Nothing exists that does not in some way contribute to spiritual enrichment in the life of the saints or help to enlarge their individual capacities to experience a much happier and more exalted life. Everything is one harmonious, progressive, interrelated whole, arranged for the purpose of bringing joy to all who have gone to Heaven—all those who have put their trust in Jesus. All who enter this beautiful city will be perfect with the bridegroom, one in love filled with all the fullness of God to live and reign with Him in glory throughout eternity (see Ephesians 3:14–21).

Satan and sin have distorted every physical capability of mankind. However, in Heaven all five senses of a Christian, free from any encumbrance, will be perfected. In our youth, the physical senses— taste, smell, sight, hearing, touch—are at their best. In Heaven, the young will have their joy increased ten thousand times, and the old will become young again.

For example, we will have a perfect sense of taste. In Heaven, unlike on Earth, we will not need to constantly partake of food to maintain our existence. On Earth, much of our time and energy is devoted to the search for and preparation of food. When the Lord placed the perfect man in the perfect Garden of Eden, he was given every herb and tree for food. When man fell, the curse made it necessary for him to acquire his bread by the sweat of his brow.

On Earth, we find pleasure in the consumption of delicious foods. In Heaven, we will be able to partake of an even greater variety and our sense of appreciation will be much more refined than any human has enjoyed on Earth.

In Heaven, our sense of smell will become more refined. A perfected order of life will include an enhanced ability to appreciate the sweetness of perfumes distilled from ten thousand flowers.

This scent will fill the entire atmosphere and provide a source of enjoyment never experienced by anyone on Earth.

Our hearing will be perfected. It has been said, "All Heaven is an unbroken perfect harmony." Music favorites and songs that we all love, as well as birds singing that we now hear imperfectly, will be heard with greater clarity and discernment, as well as an increased ability to fully appreciate each sound. In Paradise, because all ears are in tune with God, they are able to hear celestial music unlike anything ever heard by any earthly ear.

Our sight will be perfected. One of the appeals of the blind man was, *"Lord, that I might receive my sight"* (Mark 10:51). How little we see here on Earth. How blind we are to all that is going on around us. In Heaven, there is no impaired eyesight, no blurred or distorted vision. In God's country, our vision will be limitless in its range. Impaired eyes will be clarified and able to see all the loveliness and every beauty found in glory land.

Here on Earth, we almost daily pass by thousands of flowers without really seeing them. There are beautiful birds, animals— every wonder of nature—but more often than not, we walk right by them, seldom giving them so much as a second glance. Even children as they joyfully bounce and play all around us, largely go unnoticed, along with a hundred other potential pleasures that we pass by on a daily basis, too blind to see. The scenic beauty of ancient mountains is not allowed to distract our attention from the path upon which we have fixed our minds and eyes. Valleys with rippling hills or plains of daisies excite us very little. With each passing day here in Earth it seems as though the powers of darkness blind us just a little bit more. In Heaven, however, we will comment, *"Where as I was blind, now I see"* (John 9:25). There we will realize that never before have we truly seen the full beauty of a single lily. We will finally understand what the Lord meant when He said, *"Consider how the lilies grow ... Yet I tell you, not even Solomon in all his splendor was dressed like one of these"* (Luke 12:27). Praises will ring out to the Lord for every beauty that He has prepared for those who love Him.

Our soul and spirit will be perfected and will be at complete rest. The soul, never before satisfied, will be at peace. We will be in our heavenly home where our soul shall never hunger or wander anymore. We will know that we have entered a safe haven, resting in perfect peace and complete satisfaction, entirely happy and overflowing with ecstatic joy.

WE SHALL ALL BE FILLED WITH TRUE KNOWLEDGE AND GIFTED WITH PERFECT INTUITION.

On Earth we experience brief periods of time—measured in days or hours—or sometimes only momentary flashes when our minds seem unusually clear. We have periods when we are able to think clearly, but in Heaven there will be no faulty memory or confusion of thought, as no imperfection of mind ever falls upon any of God's people. Clear thinking, right thinking, deep thinking, and divine thinking are the heritage of all who dwell there.

We will also have perfect knowledge. On Earth, we "see through a glass darkly" at best. That will not be the case in Heaven. There will be a wonderful expansion of knowledge and an ability to see things in their right relationships, ones that seemed contradictory or unexplainable here on Earth. Many truths of the Bible that puzzle us now—truths over which the church on Earth continually divides and splits—will finally be seen in an appropriate light. On Earth, selfish interests are so deep-seated, preconceived ideas so entrenched, and personal prejudices so overwhelming, our reasoning power has become erroneous. In his writings, the apostle Paul, a most sincere seeker of truth, seems to say this is fact when he implies, "I see through a glass darkly. I know very little. I am picking up pebbles of truth, but every notion of undiscovered truth, what truth I do know, I am unable to fit perfectly into its proper place, in its right proportion and emphasis with all other truths."

In Heaven, we shall be free of any error. We shall all be filled with true knowledge and gifted with perfect intuition. On Earth, the honeybee knows without being taught how to build a cell that will store the largest possible amount of honey. This hexagonal cell is of such perfect geometric proportions that man has been unable to improve upon the plan, and yet the untaught bee—working in unison and perfect cooperation with others of its kind—is able to build it in the dark. This is knowledge without instruction. This is perfect cooperation, a large number of bees working with other bees to complete a task so intricate it puzzles the minds of men.

With this same perfection and in much the same way (perhaps in exactly the same way) God's entire family in Heaven, from lowest to highest, all work together. Each member carries out his or her particular duties, and an unseen power from the throne coordinates all the intellectual, emotional, and spiritual elements within each individual so that all cooperate perfectly as they follow one great plan.

There is a language in Heaven that all can speak and understand without being taught, and there is also knowledge gained without it being consciously acquired. Like the bees in the swarm, each one of us fits into the perfect plan. Each person knows what the other thinks before he speaks. By this heavenly intuition, we will recognize and know everyone in Heaven who was a friend or relative here on Earth. Without even being told, our friends will know of our arrival in Heaven, and they will come to welcome us in the parks or perhaps in the mansions. Likewise without

introduction, we shall know the patriarchs and saints in Heaven—
Abraham, Daniel, Moses, the prophets, and the apostles. We shall
recognize each one as soon as we see them, and we shall see every
one of them. There is in Heaven a higher knowledge than mankind now possesses. Here on Earth, only a fraction of that heavenly knowledge is available to us.

This intuitive sense we call instinct as it is found in all of natural creation, cannot be explained in human terms. The homing
pigeon, for example, flies over and over again to its home without
error. Year after year, the robin returns at the right season to build
its nest in the old apple tree. The oriole weaves its hanging nest and
knows how to find its food beneath the bark, and where to raise its
young in the hollow of the tree. Insects, worms, birds and beasts
all know where and how to find the proper food and how to avoid
an enemy. Hummingbirds work in pairs to build their minute
nest. Ants and bees work in colonies or swarms in perfect cooperation, building geometrically perfect homes. They cooperate in
caring for their young and in fulfilling their own perfect place in
nature without being taught, without a language or a visible way
of communicating thought. They do not think, they do not reason, yet they know. This is but an imperfect illustration of God's
great colony or swarm in the everlasting city of Heaven where His
knowledge, working in all of silent creation, will reach harmonious
perfection in everything that exists there—bird, beast, and man.
Every living creature in Heaven possesses this intuitive knowledge
according to his capacity and his position in God's economy.

In Heaven, pure love flows like a river from one individual
to the next. No one in Heaven can refrain from loving others,
everyone is so beautiful and gracious. A perfect spirit pervades all
of Heaven. There is no discord, not a rasping voice, not a motion
out of rhythm, not an ill-spoken word, nor an unkind thought.

In Heaven every one retains his earthly identity. Love, pure and undefiled, between the heavenly saints is more beautiful and thrilling than ever was love between friend, or man and woman. This love, in itself, makes all Heaven a Paradise. This holy love knows no boundaries, and it will never grow cold. In Heaven, love in its highest and purest form is a love that will stand the test of time.

GOD IS LOVE, AND SO IS HEAVEN!

All that mars the best in man is done away with in Heaven. The veil that covers the beauty in each soul is taken away. All are pure; all are perfect. God is love, and so is Heaven! There in Heaven all mankind will serve one another. There is no jealousy or even so much as an envious thought. Saints, like angels, are endowed with life from the throne. Everyone helps one another in love without envy or pride. No one will covet another's work; no one will feel his work useless.

Our heavenly homes will be situated where those people we knew and loved on Earth will surround us. We will recognize again the goodness of the Father in allowing friends to be located near each other. Everyone will be free of any racial prejudice and pride. People will be represented from every race, tribe, and tongue throughout the Earth. Though each tribe and nationality has its own characteristics, when we meet in Heaven, the love of Christ makes everyone one in heart. Though we may have differences, a common fellowship exists in Heaven, making every person feel as one with every other. In the Lord, the love bonds between those in Heaven are stronger than the bonds between race and tribe, brother and sister, or father or mother here on Earth.

Another great difference in Heaven, from what we know on Earth, is that all work will be done in the fullness and power of the Holy Spirit. Thus, the saints in Heaven, filled with the Holy Spirit, will join the angels in never-tiring, never-ending happiness, as they joyfully engage in their respective tasks.

WHAT ABOUT HELL

When I consider *what* the sacrifice of Jesus has saved us from, I would be remiss if I didn't make some comments about Hell, the other place where the souls of mankind can spend eternity.

The scriptures confirm there is a place called Hell, a destination that people do their best to ignore and really do not want to discuss, think about, or try, in any way, to comprehend. In fact, Satan and his world system have done everything possible to discount the reality of a place called Hell. The word "Hell" itself has become so commonplace when used, people have stopped associating that word with its terrible reality. In order to acquaint you with some descriptive words and phrases that will help you better understand the reality of Hell, I am going to share some thoughts stemming directly from the way I believe the Lord has chosen to lead me. In choosing where you will spend eternity—Heaven or Hell—it would be prudent to give strong consideration to the possibility of Hell and what dwelling in that place will be like.

> I WOULD BE REMISS IF I DIDN'T MAKE SOME COMMENTS ABOUT HELL.

The word "Hell" occurs fifty-four times in the Bible—thirty-one times in the Old Testament and twenty-three in the New Testament. Six times in the Gospel of Matthew alone, the Lord warns of a place called Gehenna, the final destination of the lost. In actuality, Gehenna was a deep ravine located outside the walls of Jerusalem. It was a valley where refuse from the city was dumped and eventually burned, along with the dead carcasses of criminals and a variety of other unfortunates. The Lord used it to symbolically describe final punishment for the lost so His audience could understand without difficulty what His warnings meant.

Let me warn you that there is definitely a place called Hell. We, as Christians, can be so thankful that God has provided a way for us to avoid going there. It is a terrible

LET ME WARN YOU THAT THERE IS DEFINITELY A PLACE CALLED HELL.

place of torment, excruciating pain, pitiful cries, groaning, pathetic sadness, eternal sorrow, and a level of horror beyond description. The soul of everyone in Hell will always be alive. There will be no joy, no love, no compassion, and no rest.

Fear permeates everything in Hell! Every resident trembles in a state of constant fright. There, it is impossible for anyone to find a time of peace and quiet.

In Hell, just as in Heaven, we will still have all of our senses. Sadly, the conditions of Hell are far worse than any living person can contemplate or imagine. Furthermore, there is no way out of this torturous place. There is no escape; there is no hope!

It is something like a horror movie where souls are in torment, constant agony, and despair. Jesus gave His life so that no one would have to go there. Conversely, Satan and all his demons want every person who has ever lived to spend eternity with them in Hell. That is why they fight so hard for possession of every single soul. That is why they try to deceive us concerning the reality of what the gospel represents and what the love of God has done to save mankind from this place of being lost forever in suffering and pain.

Fear grips the soul as each individual realizes they are living side by side with evil spirits and are consigned to an eternity without hope. Knowing for certain there is no way out of this place where they must coexist with the very same demons and evil spirits who torment and constantly bring them pain is, in and of itself, the source of utter despair and sorrow.

Since we are all sinners, if we have not been saved by the grace of God, pardoned by the acceptance of Jesus Christ as the one who has saved us from a burning Hell, then according to the Bible, we are bound to go there immediately when we die. **Though the flesh dies, the soul never dies.**

Luke 16:19–31 tells us Hell is a place of consciousness. Here the Lord tells about the rich man who died and then awoke in Hell. *"The rich man also died and was buried. In hell, where he was in torment, he looked up and saw Abraham far away, with Lazarus by his side. So he called to him, 'Father Abraham, have pity on me and send Lazarus to dip the tip of his finger in water and cool my tongue, because I am in agony in this fire ... send Lazarus to my father's house, for I have five brothers. Let him warn them, so that they will not also come to this place of torment.' Abraham replied, 'They have Moses and the Prophets; let them listen to them"* (Luke 16:22–24, 27–29).

In these verses the Lord provides evidence of at least ten areas in which human consciousness continues and even intensifies in Hell:

1. *"In hell, where he was in torment, he looked up and saw ..."*: He could see.
2. *"Was in torment"*: so he could feel.
3. *"Saw Abraham ... with Lazarus"*: He could recognize.
4. *"He called to him"*: He could speak.
5. *"Abraham, have pity"*: He could plead.
6. *"I am in agony in this fire"*: He could suffer.
7. *"Abraham replied... (to him)"*: He could hear.

8. *"Son, remember"* (verse 25): He had memory.

9. *"Send Lazarus to my ... brothers"*: He could reflect.

10. *"That they will not also come to this place of torment"*: He could think ahead.

Hell is terrible! In the New Testament, Jesus gives us many grave warnings about this awful place, hoping that we will be stirred to investigate and learn how we can escape the damnation of such an existence, one in which *"the flame is never quenched."*

In scripture, Jesus comments that there will be gnashing of teeth for those who choose to go to Hell.

IT HAS ALWAYS BEEN MANKIND WHO TURNED HIS BACK ON GOD.

His life was a message to a lost world that says this: *"I do not desire that you go to Hell."*

You may ask, is God really fair? More than fair! We humans seem to forget, or don't want to think about the fact that it has always been mankind who turned his back on God; God never turned against anyone. He didn't have to save us! It required a great sacrifice on the part of both God the Father and His Son, Jesus. We should be thankful He loved us enough to provide a plan to save us from spending our eternity in Hell, despite our living contrary to His standards.

God made us for His own joy and for everlasting fellowship. We are His creation, and He loves us. We can either choose to call upon Jesus and accept Him as our Savior, whereupon He will forgive us and bless us with an eternity in Heaven, or we can deny Him.

I will now explain to you how you can be sure you will spend your eternity in Heaven and avoid an eternity in Hell.

THE CHOICE IS OURS

We may choose to ignore both Heaven and Hell and the possibility that either exists. Earlier I quoted a survey stating a full eighty-eight percent of the people questioned who said they believe there is a *Heaven also believed they would be going there.* This kind of reasoning is based solely on what we want to believe—what we want to hear.

> **FAILURE TO CHOOSE**
>
> **IS A CHOICE!**

In reality, the God who created the universe, Earth, and all of mankind, is the only one who has the authority to make that decision. It is His desire that everyone should be saved; He wants no one to be lost. He paid a tremendous price so that no one would be lost. However, He also gave mankind freedom of choice. He did not create robots. All of us will live forever in one of two places. We will spend eternity in one place or the other. The choice is ours.

God has revealed this information very plainly in His Word, which He has miraculously preserved for mankind down through the ages so that we will know. His message has been made available using the written word as well as the spoken word of those who preach and teach from the Bible. Each individual must make a choice. Failure to choose is a choice!

However large and pressing the questions related to our present brief existence on this Earth, they become totally irrelevant when compared with the subject of death and our life in the hereafter. No matter how wise people may like to believe they are, if they do not inquire about the hereafter, they are fools. Death is a stark reality. It cannot be avoided. To act wisely is to face it head on with eyes wide open.

There are millions of people who show little or no interest, and other millions who are deeply concerned but misdirected as a result of false teaching and mistaken ideas about life after death. In actuality, the Bible—the Word of God—is the only authority available to us that can be fully trusted. I believe it is the inspired Word of the only true and living God. All other presentations are based on the mental reasoning of mankind. And, even if you disagree, it only makes good sense for anyone, at the very least, to consider the Bible as a resource that cannot be dismissed or ignored. The consequences are too great.

It is easy, as well as sensible, to believe a Supreme Being created the universe and the life of every living creature. If, as some profess, we just evolved out of matter, how then did we develop thought? How did such emotions as love, hate, hope, fear, joy, sorrow, etc., develop out of insensible matter? How did physical atoms and electrical impulses produce a moral conscience in humans? If we evolved randomly, how did the amazing gender differences in males and females develop and become so uniquely perfect they are able to reproduce? Or, for that matter, why isn't life on Earth now being partially replenished, both human and nonhuman, by more new creatures still evolving rather than exclusively by a gender-specific reproduction system involving male and female?

The soul, that nonmaterial, indefinable substance which is the real you, the real me, outlives all physical change. Even though the physical body dies or ceases to function, no one has yet been able to supply evidence that the real person, the spiritual soul, actually disintegrates or does not live on forever.

A million graveyards tell us that death is man's greatest problem. Death is no respecter of humankind. The words *"Till death do us part"* ring out in every wedding ceremony. With every passing minute, several people pass from this present life on Earth into the life hereafter. The fact that there is life after death is confirmed in nearly every part of the Bible. **Therefore, it is imperative that I explore with you the biblical way that will definitely lead you to Heaven.**

The true God of Heaven is a loving and just God, who *"wants all men to be saved and to come to a knowledge of the truth"* (I Timothy 2:4). As we begin our search for the way that will definitely lead us to Heaven, it becomes almost immediately apparent there are many different approaches to religion in general, as well as to Christianity itself. We need to know the difference, so the one we choose will not mislead us, but will definitely show us the way to Heaven.

Even true biblical Christianity is not always portrayed accurately by secular society or, for that matter, by every church. The *"knowledge of the truth"* the Bible refers to in I Timothy 2:4 is given in the very next verse, as well as several others in the New Testament:

"For there is one God and one mediator between God and men, the man Christ Jesus" (I Timothy 2:5).

A few of the others include:

- *"Whoever believes in him is not condemned, but whoever does not believe stands condemned already because he has not believed in the name of God's one and only Son"* (John 3:16–18).
- *"Yet to all who received him,* (referring to Jesus Christ) *to those who believed in his name, he gave the right to become children of God—children born not of natural descent, nor of human decision or a husband's will, but born of God"* (John 1:12–13).
- *"And this is the testimony: God has given us eternal life, and this life is in his Son. He who has the Son has life; he who does not have the Son of God does not have life"* (1 John 5:11–12).

All of the teachings of the Bible direct us to true Christianity—the gospel of Jesus Christ. In turn, that gospel leads us, as individuals, to a personal encounter—a personal relationship—with Jesus Christ as Savior and Lord. That is the essence of true biblical Christianity! That is the only truth that you can know for sure will take you to Heaven.

Though we may not fully understand all that happens in the spiritual world, it is the acceptance of God's Son, Jesus Christ, as our personal Savior that triggers the release of God's power in our lives. At that very moment, we experience an event often referred to as being "born again." As Jesus explained to Nicodemus in the third chapter of John, He was not referring to a physical rebirth, but to a spiritual rebirth. As the Bible states in several places, the Spirit of God literally takes up residence within our being. For example, *"Don't you know that you yourselves are God's temple and that God's Spirit lives in you?"* (1 Corinthians 3:16).

THAT IS THE ONLY TRUTH THAT YOU CAN KNOW FOR SURE WILL TAKE YOU TO HEAVEN.

When we accept Jesus Christ as our personal savior, the one who can save us from Hell because of the sacrifice He made on our behalf, immediately, we become children of the one true God, children who will spend eternity with Him in that special place called Heaven that He has lovingly prepared for us.

Unfortunately, however, there is also a second kind of Christianity in the world—one I call the religion of Christianity. Although it is not based on biblical principles, it is a form of Christianity many people passionately practice and believe in. It directs our faith towards manmade concepts and practices, just like the religion of Israel was practicing when Jesus walked with us here on Earth. A Christian commitment to "things," "doctrines," "ordinances," "traditions," "structures," and "personalities" can never pass the test of true biblical Christian teachings. Our commitment cannot be to anything or anyone other than Jesus Christ and His teachings as found in the scriptures. This unbiblical type of Christianity has caused much confusion. Even more importantly it could very well cause people to **miss** Heaven.

I would never point anyone in the direction of some weak-kneed, shallow form of Christianity that is anything other than the true way. **Heaven is far too valuable for that.** I am talking about a commitment that leads to something much more valuable than gold, silver, diamonds, or anything else this world might have to offer.

In today's Christian environment, it is easy for us to become involved, but that alone does not automatically mean we are committed to Jesus Christ and all of His teachings. There is a vast difference between the two. It is very easy to become involved; involvement only denotes activity. People can be active in a church without being transformed by Jesus Christ. Many in fact, are committed to a lot of different causes and popular philosophies. They could even be doing many good works in the name of Jesus. However, that does not automatically mean they have experienced a personal relationship with Him. The importance of that relationship cannot be overstated. The apostle Paul was involved on a full-time basis in the religion of his day—even a leader—but he said, *"Whatever was to my profit I now consider loss for the sake of Christ. What is more, I consider everything a loss compared to the surpassing greatness of knowing Christ Jesus my Lord, for whose sake I have lost all things. I consider them rubbish, that I may gain Christ and be found in Him, not having a righteousness of my own that comes from the law* (being able to keep all of the commandments) *but that which is through faith in Christ"* (Philippians 3:7–9).

Jesus Christ was the true and living God in the flesh, the very same God who created all things, including you and me. When the virgin Mary gave birth to Jesus, an angel said to the shepherds who were living out in the fields near His birthplace of Bethlehem, *"Do not be afraid. I bring you good news of great joy that will be for all the people. Today in the town of David* (that was

Bethlehem) *a Savior has been born to you; he is Christ the Lord. This will be a sign to you: You will find a baby wrapped in cloths and lying in a manger.' Suddenly a great company of the heavenly host appeared with the angel, praising God and saying, 'Glory to God in the highest, and on earth peace to men on whom his favor rests'"* (Luke 2:10–14).

Jesus became the Savior for all who willingly come to Him. He is both willing and able to save their souls from Hell. The angels knew how important this would be for all of mankind. To them, it was good news of great joy indeed!

The ministry of Jesus Christ only lasted about three and one-half years, yet the effect of His life on the history of mankind has been far greater than anyone else who ever lived.

Consider the following truths—earlier, I touched on some of them:

- Jesus lived in poverty and was reared in obscurity.
- He received no formal education and never possessed wealth or widespread societal influence.
- He did not travel extensively. Only once did He cross the boundary of the country where He lived.
- In infancy, He startled a king. In childhood, He puzzled doctors. In manhood, He ruled the course of nature, walked upon the waves, and hushed the sea to sleep.
- He never wrote a book. Yet His life has inspired more books than that of any other human being.
- He never wrote a song. Yet He has furnished the theme for more songs than all the songwriters combined who ever lived.
- He never gathered an army, nor drafted a soldier, nor used a weapon. He never fired a shot. Yet no leader ever had more rebels surrender to Him.

Many great statesmen have come and gone. Even scientists, philosophers, and theologians are soon forgotten. But the reputation of this Man continues to change lives.

One day of each and every week, the wheels of commerce slow down, and multitudes gather to pay homage and show Him respect. His enemies could not destroy Him, and the grave could not hold Him.

Have you ever wondered why Jesus has had so much influence? He was God on Earth in the form of a human being. If you really want to know God, just look at the life of Jesus Christ.

Jesus said, "*No one comes to the Father except through me*" (John 14:6).

One of the greatest obstacles human beings face in becoming a biblical Christian is the deep-seated belief that they can never be good enough. Or because they see sin in the lives of Christians, they completely dismiss the possibility that Christian teachings could show them the way to God. Does that kind of thinking sound familiar? If it does, inaccurate information is probably the cause.

DOES THAT KIND OF THINKING SOUND FAMILIAR?

You buy into this conclusion, even though it is false, because you don't understand true biblical Christianity and have failed to fully comprehend what God has done for you.

In theory, you are right if you believe you can't be good enough. No one is ever good enough. Piling up brownie points in the hope they will somehow make you acceptable in God's sight is a futile effort. It can't be done! In fact, that is the Good News of the Gospel of Jesus Christ. Our salvation is not based on our individual ability to be good enough, to be sinless. Rather it is based upon the righteousness of Jesus Christ. This is what the Bible means when it says, *"Salvation is found in no one else, for there is no other name under heaven given to men by which we must be saved"* (Acts 4:12).

Jesus is the only individual who was ever good enough to qualify for citizenship in Heaven. He alone lived a sinless life. By accepting Him as our personal Savior, people like you and me are immediately made right with God— that is the only way we can lay hold of the righteousness we need. That is why *"salvation is found in no one else"* as the above verse states. When we believe in and accept Jesus as our personal Savior, His righteousness is credited to our account in the eyes of God. This is good news indeed!

Listen to this: *"But now a righteousness from God, apart from law* (our keeping all of God's commandments) *has been made known, to which the Law and the Prophets testify.* **This righteousness from God comes through faith in Jesus Christ to all who believe** (accept Him as their Savior—emphasis added). *There is no difference, for all have sinned and fall short of the glory of God, and are justified freely by his grace* **(our salvation is a free gift)** *through the redemption that came by Christ Jesus. God presented him as a sacrifice of atonement, through faith in his blood"* (Romans 3:21–25).

> HIS RIGHTEOUSNESS IS CREDITED TO OUR ACCOUNT IN THE EYES OF GOD.

God can't ignore sin and pretend it doesn't exist. Neither can He look at the evil in each of our lives and contrive an excuse for it. Instead of turning His back on mankind, which He had a right to do, because of His great love for us, He devised a plan that would be completely fair and would nullify the power and consequences sin holds over us. He sent us His Son Jesus to rescue us and redeem us from Hell. This was accomplished for all mankind when the life of Jesus was exchanged as full payment for all of our sins. For those who will believe and receive this offer from God, He does a wonderful thing: He justifies us. *"Know that a man is not justified by observing the law, but by faith in Jesus Christ because by observing the law* (always keeping God's commandments) *no one will be justified"* (Galatians 2:16).

Everyone knows down deep they don't match up to the standards of God. Because one of the characteristics of God is to be completely fair and honest in all things, He can't change His standards in order to justify us. That is why the only way the penalty of sin in our lives can be removed is by believing in and receiving His son Jesus as our Savior. When we do, God then does a wonderful thing: He deposits the righteousness of Jesus Christ into our personal account. That is how our relationship with God is altered so we fit His standards, which then qualifies us for an eternal home in Heaven. No one can ever be good enough of themselves, because we are born spiritually with a self-centered sinful nature (see Romans 5:6–20 and 7:14–24 through 8:1–4).

Do we deserve this? Absolutely not! It is God's grace, found only in the person of Jesus Christ that makes this marvelous gift of salvation from Hell available to us. It is a gift from God, and it is absolutely free. Finally, and best of all, it assures us of an eternity in Heaven.

How are you going to respond to such a gift? The Bible says there is a day of final judgment coming, and on that day every person who has ever lived will be judged individually according to the way they have chosen to exercise their own free will in the conduct of their lives. It says those who are not believers in the gospel of Jesus Christ are condemned: *"Whoever believes in him is not condemned, but whoever does not believe stands condemned already because he has not believed in the name of God's one and only Son"* (John 3:18).

That is a fearful thought! Every human being should stop, listen, and consider while this opportunity still lingers. Be done with perilous procrastination. Personally, I believe more souls will be lost to the lake of fire as the result of procrastination than for any other reason.

I have no desire to play on your emotions. I am simply trying to address your intelligence, conscience, and free will in a forthright manner. Death has a way of striking unexpectedly, and with it, the last chance is gone, never to be repeated. There is no "second chance." Receive the risen Lord and living Savior Jesus Christ into your heart right now, without delay. Possessing Him is the only way you can be sure of going to Heaven and being saved from spending eternity in Hell.

> BE DONE WITH PERILOUS PROCRASTINATION.

For me, discussing the ramifications of death is not a morbid pastime. It is every bit as rational as it is inescapable. Soon enough we all must pass over to the other side of the grave. For all of us who know the Lord Jesus as our Savior, the grave has been transformed from a foe to a friend. With the Bible to back us up, we can say with complete confidence, "We need have no fear of death." It will be a wonderful experience. Our last breath here will coincide with a healing that is both instantaneous and complete, fully supplemented by an exquisite form of joy that can only be experienced on the other side in Heaven. Jesus and Heaven are ours! In a word, sunset here is sunrise there. Paul said, *"For to me, to live is Christ and to die is gain"* (Philippians 1:21).

Nothing bankrupts humans so completely as death. To the unsaved person, death is the final pauperizing blow, the super-loss. In an instant, every thrill and ambition is extinguished.

What a contrast to Paul's statement: *"To die is gain."* Only a Christian, which is what Paul became, could make this statement with such utter certainty and mean it based on certified guarantees. He knew, as we can, the basis of our hope in the Christian faith is factually sound.

Paul encountered the risen Jesus, in person, on the road to Damascus. Subsequently, he searched the sacred scriptures with scholarly care and discovered the birth, life, miracles, death, resurrection, and ascension of Jesus all clearly foretold centuries in advance by the Hebrew prophets. He was convinced Jesus had fulfilled these prophecies. That knowledge and more was what prompted his cry of victory, *"To die is gain."*

The reasons why death is gain to all those who know Jesus Christ as their Savior are many. To them what Heaven represents is unique and unmistakable. It means the very highest fulfillment of all pure hopes, ageless vitality, and every sorrow healed. Gone forever will be the burden of mortal flesh and earthly troubles, weakness, pain, temptation, grief, limitation, and frustration. Heaven is a place where there is no unholy thought, desire, fear, doubt, or anxiety. No more hungering and thirsting, every tear wiped away, drinking "living waters" of immortality. The transition from here to there will be fabulous: from this to that, from now to then. Peter describes it as *"an inheritance incorruptible, and undefiled, and that fadeth not away"* (I Peter 1:4).

All around us will be those shining "clouds of witnesses"— the redeemed of all the centuries, all serving the same Savior and all with pure hearts welcoming our participation. Moses, David, John, Paul, and perhaps even Peter himself will interject, *"Ye rejoice with joy unspeakable and full of glory"* (I Peter 1:8 KJV).

Add to all that the pleasure of a reunion with our departed loved ones who were near and dear to us in this present world. Their physical identities will be exactly the same as when they were here with us, except every wrinkle, every blemish, every disfigurement, and every mark of age or weakness will have been taken away forever. Identities will not be faded and personalities will not be blurred. You will always be you. I shall always be me.

For some, the fate of young children who die is an important concern. I believe the Bible implies they are not lost. Yes, from birth everyone is sin-infected (see Romans 5:12–19). However, they are not guilty, as ignorance absolves or sets them free of any responsibility. They are not saved by their innocence, but they are saved because of it. I believe the Bible teaches we do not become responsible for our transgressions until we reach a responsible age. It is at that point when everyone becomes a transgressor and, as a consequence, must shoulder the responsibility for the associated guilt.

When we do reach the age of responsibility, each of us will have a choice we must make. Will it be Heaven or Hell? Either way, this choice will be for eternity; it will never ever end. That is why I ask you not to procrastinate—make the wise choice now. Many people try to avoid this choice by closing their ears, but one way or another, they are making it even if it is by their silence. No one can escape this truth regardless of how hard they try.

There are those people who prefer to just ignore reality and the fact they will ultimately have to make such a choice. They would rather not think about it. Then there are people, who have convinced themselves neither Heaven nor Hell really exist and, based on this premise, declare the need for any choice totally irrelevant. Furthermore, as I referred to earlier, according to a poll in USA TODAY, most people who believe there is a Heaven also believed they would be going there. This is their stated belief, even though they have made no effort to find out what conditions or requirements might apply. Why people use these and other kinds of

haphazard rationalizations in order to ease their conscience or justify a faulty choice is difficult for me to always comprehend.

Given even the slightest possibility that Heaven and Hell exist, it
is far too critical of a decision for anyone to pass off lightly, and at the
very least, realize good sense demands they give the subject serious
consideration. Dismissing or ignoring the subject by not trying to find
out all that it involves, without any research, is poor judgment. This is
especially true when the potential consequences are eternal in nature.

> You do not want to **miss** Heaven.
> God does not want you to **miss** Heaven.
> I do not want you to **miss** Heaven.
> You do not *have* to **miss** Heaven.

Let me again briefly review how you can be sure you don't miss
Heaven. The Bible makes it very clear that none of us—beginning
from the time we are born—could
ever be good enough to qualify for
Heaven. It is because of our spiritual heritage, which began with the
disobedience of Adam and Eve, we
are (so to speak) spiritually born on
the wrong side of the tracks. I am
sure you wish—I know I do—this
was not the fact. However, according to the Bible, that is our spiritual condition, so we are in need of a Savior who has the power
to rescue us. Otherwise, we would all be doomed to an eternity
in Hell. The name of that Savior is Jesus Christ. What qualified
Him to be mankind's Savior is His coming to Earth and living a
sinless life, then offering this sinless life up to God on the cross
as a sacrifice for the sins of all mankind. This is how He, in fact,

> GIVEN EVEN THE
> SLIGHTEST POSSIBILITY
> THAT HEAVEN AND
> HELL EXIST

positioned Himself to deliver us from the fate we so justly deserve.

I trust this brief explanation helps you understand *why* God's plan for our salvation demands we believe in His Son Jesus and accept Him as our Savior. By doing so, this allows God to credit the sinless life of Jesus to our life. It is this credit alone that serves as full payment for our ticket to Heaven. If that isn't good news, I don't know what is! Mankind has no authority to alter God's plan, or adopt any other that is humanly developed, nor should they want to, because it can't work. Only God's plan is indeed perfect, making wise the simple, as it is with all things from God.

You may ask, is God's plan really fair? In response, I would argue it is more than fair! It required an unthinkable sacrifice on the part of both God the Father and His Son, Jesus. When you consider the fact mankind has always been the viola-

> **THIS ALLOWS GOD TO CREDIT THE SINLESS LIFE OF JESUS TO OUR LIFE.**

tor of every failed covenant with God, this plan could not have been more magnanimous. We should be thankful that He loved each of us enough to even offer such a plan. God didn't have to save us! However, through His plan, despite the fact that our behavior does not always match his standards, we can find safe haven from an eternity in Hell.

Let us pause for a minute to look at this subject where you will spend eternity from a different perspective. **Consider with me a simple exercise in logic ...**

First, let us assume you are a person who believes there is a place called Heaven and you also believe, as does the majority, that Heaven is where you will spend eternity after you die. Next, let us assume you are right. Finally, ask yourself what possible harm could come from doing as the Bible says you must, and accept Jesus Christ as your personal Savior?

On the other hand, if you are wrong, and the Bible is right—if you refuse to comply with God's plan of salvation and only those who accept Jesus Christ as their personal Savior go to Heaven—then your choice *not* to accept Jesus Christ will be devastating for all eternity.

The first option has the potential for terrible consequences. But the second option to accept the Gospel of Jesus Christ as presented in the Bible is without risk. That choice won't harm you, even if it proves to be unnecessary, while the other, if incorrect, carries the risk of an eternity in Hell for your soul.

We must all choose one option or the other. Using pure logic, which is the wise choice? Only you can make that choice. Like it or not, that single choice will decide your circumstances for eternity. That may sound harsh, but it is the unvarnished truth.

GOD KNOWS YOUR HEART.

Every person is valuable to God. He loves you in spite of the terrible things you may have done in your life leading up to this point in time. He wants everyone to recognize and fully understand the truth. No one could have been more guilty of sin than the apostle Paul before he learned the truth about Jesus Christ.

Repent (which is to decide in your heart to change your way of thinking) and accept Jesus Christ into your heart as your Savior and Lord. That is what Paul did and what millions have done since. It's the only sure way to know you are going to Heaven. If you are sincere and mean it from the heart, you will experience a spiritual rebirth. It is not necessary to understand what this all means. You will know that it happened, and the Bible says you will be in the Kingdom of God and on your way to Heaven, *"For he has rescued us from the dominion of darkness and brought us into the kingdom of the Son he loves, in whom we have redemption, the forgiveness of sins"* (Colossians 1:13–14).

God knows your heart. He's not nearly as concerned with your words as He is with the attitude of your heart. Let me suggest a simple prayer if you really want to accept Jesus as your Lord and Savior: "Lord Jesus, I want to know You personally. Thank You for sacrificing Your life on the cross for my sins. I open the door of my heart and receive You as my Savior and Lord. Thank You for forgiving me of my sins and making it possible for me to spend my eternal life in Heaven. Take control of the throne of my life and make me the kind of person You want me to be."

You may very well think this approach is too simple. That's because the mind of mankind has chosen to make it complicated—not God. If this prayer expresses the desire of your heart and you mean it, offer it up to God—right now, don't put it off— and Christ will come into your life, just as He has promised.

It is important that you locate a church that believes in and tries to replicate true biblical Christianity, so you can become well grounded in the Word of God and be actively engaged in Christian fellowship. It will bring you great joy and happiness, not the drudgery and lack of fun that Satan's kingdom—society—wants the public to believe is normal fare in the life of a committed Christian. Of course, there will be spiritual battles as Satan tries to deceive or hurt anyone who becomes a member of God's Kingdom. However, as the Bible has promised, you will be equipped with the Holy Spirit to guide your way and give you the spiritual strength to prevail in these battles. I can tell you this based on personal experience. It is not a mere talking point.

Look at these scriptures. Jesus said:

"And I will ask the Father, and he will give you another Counselor to be with you forever—the Spirit of truth (speaking of the Holy Spirit) ... *you know him, for he lives with you and will be in you"* (John 14:16–17).

"Now I am going to him who sent me ... But I tell you the truth: It is for your good that I am going away (Jesus speaking of returning to Heaven after His resurrection). *Unless I go away, the Counselor* (Holy Spirit) *will not come to you; but if I go, I will send him to you"* (John 16:7).

After Jesus ascended to Heaven, Peter was preaching and said, *"God has raised this Jesus to life, and we are all witnesses of the fact ... he has received from the Father the promised Holy Spirit ... God has made this Jesus ... both Lord and Christ. When the people heard this, they were cut to the heart and said to Peter and the other apostles, 'Brothers, what shall we do?' Peter replied, 'Repent and be baptized, every one of you, in the name of Jesus Christ so that your sins may be forgiven.* **And you will receive the gift of the Holy Spirit'"** (Acts 2:32, 33, 36–38—emphasis added).

> THE SINGLE MOST IMPORTANT DIFFERENCE BETWEEN TRUE CHRISTIANITY AND ALL OTHER RELIGIONS.

Several passages in the New Testament tell us that all Christians become a temple of the Holy Spirit. I would like to draw your attention to one of them that I referenced before: *"Don't you know that you yourselves are God's temple and that God's Spirit lives in you?"* (I Corinthians 3:16)

This fact that the Holy Spirit lives within our heart after we are born again is the single most important difference between true Christianity and all other religions. Only those who receive Jesus Christ as their Lord and Savior—receive the promised Holy Spirit— are reborn spiritually. The Bible teaches only those who have the Holy Spirit living within them will be raised up to Heaven: *"And if the Spirit of him who raised Jesus from the dead is living in you, he who raised Christ from the dead will also give life to your mortal bodies through his Spirit, who lives in you"* (Romans 8:11).

The Bible promises eternal life in Heaven to all who receive Christ: *"And this is the testimony: God has given us eternal life, and this life is in his Son. He who has the Son has life; he who does not have the Son of God does not have life. I write these things to you who believe in the name of the Son of God so that you may know that you have eternal life"* (I John 5:11–13).

Jesus Christ set us free from the effects of sin, and He has set us free from the effects coming from the power of the world and our self-centered sinful nature. John 8:36 tells us that whoever the Son has set free is free indeed. However, keep in mind that being delivered from the condemning effect of our sinful nature is different from being free of the world's power to tempt us with its ways and standards. That is a process! In several areas of your life, it will not happen immediately. Paul's experience in Romans 7:14—8:4 after he became a Christian is a case in point.

We have come to the end of our spiritual adventure. I believe there are many committed Christians with a deep desire to know the Lord more intimately. I hope you are one of them. I have purposed in the message of this book to inform you how our spiritual enemy, working through our worldly society, is doing all within his power to keep us from fulfilling our mission to be this world's salt and light.

Up front I warned you this message would not be anything like a pleasure jaunt ... a Christian cruise with breakfast served in your stateroom. Instead, it was designed to be a time for accelerated, measurable, and lasting spiritual growth.

I hope you take full advantage of this opportunity. In every chapter, I tried to challenge your intellect and encourage a critical analysis of everything you claim to believe, even if it took you outside of your spiritual comfort zone. Hopefully, you have been diligent to listen carefully to what God, through His Holy Spirit, has been saying to your heart.

Will the effects of this message be lasting? Only you can answer that question. It is my prayerful hope the powerful truths we have discussed during this spiritual adventure will continue to enlighten you and not be soon forgotten—that they will result in a lifelong transformation.

More specifically, if God grants any of us an extension of life as we presently know it—ten, twenty, thirty years or more—in a world I fearfully believe will be quite unlike the one we now know, may He still find us practicing the presence of Jesus the Christ, the anointed of God, joyfully declaring, "He is risen—I remain totally committed to Him and believe His coming will be timely and very soon."

How goes the world? Our world goes not well … But the Kingdom comes!

The Lord gave me the following word to help guide my path in serving Him.

"DO NOT FEAR THE DAYS AHEAD,
BUT FEAR THIS ONLY: THAT YOU
WALK IN A MANNER PLEASING TO THE LORD."
AMEN!

MAY GOD BLESS YOU AND MAY GOD BLESS
AMERICA WITH A HOLY SPIRIT-LED REVIVAL.

Will You Help Us (Not Financially) Share This Message?

This book, *Revival or Judgment*, retails for $11.95, the necessary price to cover cost at the retail level. Christian Life Outreach has the funds to send you up to *ten copies* of this book for a total cost of only $10.00 to share a copy with your relatives, friends, church members, and neighbors. The price of $10.00 is the same for any number of copies between one and ten. If you are able to share more than ten copies, add $1.00 to the $10.00 for each additional copy you order over ten. We only ask you to help us with our postage and handling cost.

In addition, regardless of the number of *Revival or Judgment* copies you order, with your order we will send you one *free* copy of the book, *The Blessings of Obedience*, which retails for $9.95. This book is the testimony of Bob Fraley, the author of *Revival or Judgment*, detailing how the Lord has led him and his wife and their family during the last forty years.

His book, *You Are Salt & Light: Equipping Christians For These Last Days,* which retails for $12.95, is available to you at our ministry price of $6.00 per copy. Other options of ordering his books at our ministry price are listed on the order form. All of his books and booklets can be found at www.bobfraleychristianlifeoutreach.com.

We plan to have the last chapter of this book *What We Hope for is Coming … Don't Miss It* printed in a 32 page full color booklet. If you would have an interest for copies, let us know, we will send them to you no charge. All we ask is for you to pay the postage charge. It is listed on the order form.

Christian Life Outreach is a non-profit ministry that has several different projects. Several of these are listed on page four. We supply all of our books at a ministry price, as we only ask for you to help cover a portion of our cost.

PLEASE REFER TO THE ORDER FORM ON THE LAST PAGE OF THIS BOOK TO ORDER ANY OF BOB FRALEY'S BOOKS.

We want to share with you a few Individual responses from those who have read *The Blessings of Obedience* the testimony of Bob Fraley, author of *Revival or Judgment*, and his wife Barbara:

- "Dear Bob Fraley, thank you for the book *The Blessings of Obedience.* I read it and will pass it on to my Southern Baptist minister. Enclosed check is for a copy of *You Are Salt & Light.*"
- Tracy wrote, "Thank you for the book … I will be sending it to all my family, friends, and pastors I know."
- Katie said, "Got your book, read it in two days, and took it tonight to church and gave it to my pastor."
- In her letter, Thelma said, "I've enjoyed your book so much, read it twice, and now loaned it to a friend."
- One woman wrote she was so blessed by the book she ordered several copies to share with family and friends.
- Esther wrote, "Your book is truly revolutionary and thought provoking. I've never read a book that kept my heart pounding all the way to the end. I told my son and husband about the book, and they want to read it too. I'd like to read *Salt & Light.*"

- Henry shared, "Dear Mr. Fraley, this book *The Blessings of Obedience* has really captured our hearts and minds.
- In a letter to other pastors, Tommy and Luke Barnett of Phoenix First Assembly, one of the largest churches in America, wrote: "Not long ago we distributed over 1,500 copies of Bob Fraley's book *The Blessings of Obedience* to our church families. We also passed out more than 3,000 copies at our annual pastors' conference. This book has been an incredible blessing to so many people."

A Few Words from the Lord
Can Change Your Life Forever

Realize the Blessings of Obedience

Follow this remarkable true life story of how the Lord led two ordinary people for the saving of their family in these troubled prophetic times called The Last Days.

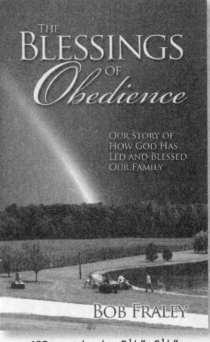

Many of the problems facing families today have been avoided by the Fraley family because God has honored and blessed their obedience. By their actions and choices, they have demonstrated (showing is always better than educational telling) what it means to live a life of faith and trust in God.

195-page book   5¼" x 8¼"

Their story is an inspiration and an example of what a person and a family can accomplish when God is at the center of everything they do and think. It is an inspirational model for us all—to be quiet and receptive to the God who speaks.

Today the Fraley family numbers 76 with children and spouses, grandchildren and spouses, great-grandchildren and continues to grow. They all, except those too young, have accepted Jesus Christ as their Savior and Lord.

Retail price $9.95
Ministry price individual order: $5. (S/H) for one book;
$6. (S/H) for each set of four books.

www.bobfraleychristianlifeoutreach.com

You Are Salt & Light

EQUIPPING CHRISTIANS FOR THESE LAST DAYS

THIS BOOK IS A MUST READ FOR ANYONE INTERESTED IN KNOWING HOW TO BE EQUIPPED FOR THESE LAST DAYS.

The biblical principles the Lord taught the Fraleys prepared them for living during these times of spiritual warfare in America.

Bob Fraley shares these Scriptural principles in *"You Are Salt & Light"* that will equip you to live victoriously and be Salt & Light in these Last Days. Discussion questions included.

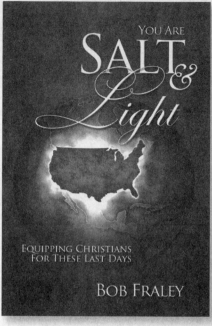

230-page book   6"x 9"

WHAT OTHERS SAY:

Every couple of years a book will profoundly affect both my thinking and living. You Are Salt & Light by Bob Fraley was that way. I was forced to grapple with thought I had never before considered, and I felt staggered by their implications. —DR. DAVID MAINS, Director of Chapel of the Air for 20 years and author of over 20 Christian books.

This book carries a powerful message. I truly believe God will use it to spark a new awakening in the church. I thoroughly recommend it. —TOMMY BARNETT, Pastor of Phoenix First Assembly of God, one of the largest churches in America and founder of the Dream Centers.

If I were to write a book, this book says everything that I would want to say. I support Bob in every way I can to get his message out. —LARRY NEVILLE, Pastor and President of Praise Chapel Fellowship, which has over 1500 churches worldwide.

Retail price $12.95
Ministry price: $6. (S/H) for one book.

www.bobfraleychristianlifeoutreach.com

ORDER FORM:

Quantity	Title	Total

SPECIAL OFFERS

____ *Revival or Judgment,* one to ten copies $10.00,
add $1.00 for each copy over ten.
*A complimentary copy of *The Blessings of Obedience* will be included
regardless of the quantity ordered. _____

____ Both *The Blessings of Obedience* and *You Are Salt & Light*
$8 S&H for each set of 2 books _____

CHURCH OFFER

____ Free copies of *The Blessings of Obedience,* for each family in my church.
A pastor must order these directly from Christian Life Outreach. (S&H free)

SEPARATE ITEMS

____ *The Blessings of Obedience,* Retail value $9.95
Our ministry price, $5 each for S&H or $6 S&H for each set of four books _____

____ *You Are Salt & Light,* Retail value $12.96
Our ministry price, $6 each for S&H _____

BOOKLETS

____ *What We Hope for is Coming...Don't Miss It,* booklet _____

____ *Rethinking Revelation Chapter 13,* booklet _____

____ *A Time for Action,* booklet _____

____ *Campaign Save Christian America,* booklet _____

All booklets: minimum order 15 each title, $3.00 for each order of 15 for S&H

S&H prices are to cover shipping & handling   S&H _____

Total _____

CIRCLE PAYMENT METHOD:

Cash   Check   Visa   MasterCard   AmEx   Discover

Card #_____ Exp. Date _____ Signature _____

Name _____

Address _____

City _____ State _____ Zip _____

If your shipping address is different from your credit card address:

Name _____

Address _____

City _____ State _____ Zip _____

Your Email Address (optional) _____

Order online at www.bobfraleychristianlifeoutreach.com

Call Toll Free: 866-998-4136   Mail: Christian Life Outreach, PO Box 31129, Phoenix, AZ 85046-1129

www.bobfraleychristianlifeoutreach.com